Surprise Box

Make the giving of a gift certificate or cash fun by presenting it in a creative manner! As the recipient removes the lid from the box, bottle caps spell out your message and the gift is clipped to the end.

Birthday Box

by Gail Ellspermann

MATERIALS:
Design Originals (13 Aqua Bottle Caps, Stickers: #0674 Red Alphabet, #0675 Blue Alphabet; #0676 All American paper) • 2½" x 3½" Paper mache box • 2 Copper eyelets • 20 jump rings • Tiny clothespin • 18 gauge colored wire • Canvas ribbon • Blue acrylic paint Purple glitter glue • Tacky glue • *USArtQuest* Perfect Paper Adhesive (PPA)

INSTRUCTIONS:

Box: Paint the top of box Blue. Let dry. Adhere a canvas ribbon around the box lid rim with Tacky glue.
• Cover bottom of box with paper using PPA.
Caps: Flatten all the caps.
• Make 2 holes in each cap.
• Link bottle caps together using jump rings.
• Add glitter glue inside the cap rim. Let dry. Add letter stickers to both sides of the caps.
Box handle: Punch 2 small holes in the lid. Set eyelets. • Twist several strands of wire together. Form a loop at each end. Wrap the wire ends with another wire.
Attach handle: Cut a 3" wire. Thread it through the loop in the handle. Push both ends through an eyelet. Twist the ends and curl inside the lid to secure. Repeat for the other side of the handle.
Attach cap string: Inside the lid, insert a jump ring into each loop. Add jump rings so the first bottle cap is below rim of the lid. Attach cap chain to the jump rings. Add a clothespin to the end of the "happy" chain.

Decorating Bottle Caps

COLOR CAPS by applying paint, nail polish, permanent marker or alcohol ink to cap (optional).

PUNCH IMAGES or photos (glued to a scrap of cardstock) with a 1" round punch.

ADD AN IMAGE by simply applying a sticker, photo, rub-on or image to the center of a cap.

GLAZE: Cover the image with a layer of clear nail polish or Diamond Glaze.

A CLEAR PEBBLE: Place a clear pebble sticker on the photo or sticker image.

ZOTS: Mash 3 zots into a cap and melt with a heat gun. Dip in embossing powder and heat (repeat).

Gail Ellspermann

Arty Doll

This fun little doll would look great as a magnet, or as a decoration on your computer monitor.

Add a pin back and it becomes a unique accessory.

Mona Lisa Doll

by Gail Ellspermann

MATERIALS:
Design Originals (Bottle Caps: 1 Navy Blue, 1 Black; Stickers: #0669 Vintage Children, #1212 Art Elements) • Black 18 gauge wire • 4 jump rings • Charms (hands, shoes) • White cardstock • *Impression Obsession* Eiffel Tower rubber stamp • *Tsukineko* StazOn Black ink • *Krylon* Copper leafing pen • 1/16" hole punch • E6000

INSTRUCTIONS:
Body: Stamp the Eiffel Tower on cardstock with Black ink. Cut it out. Line the edge with Copper leafing.
Punch a hole in the bottom of the Tower for each shoe. Attach shoe charms to the tower with jump rings.
Wrap a wire around the neck leaving long ends for arms. Slide a hand charm on each wire end and coil wire to secure.
Bottle caps: Paint the flange of the Black bottle cap with a Copper leafing pen. Flatten the Navy Blue cap. Add stickers.
Adhere caps to tower for face and body with E6000.

Bottle Cap Tinting Techniques
by Laura Dehart

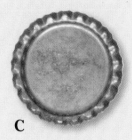

A   B   C

A Tint bottle caps with *Jacquard* Pinata alcohol inks.
B Color bottle cap with a Black Sharpie marker.
C Apply Metallic Rub-Ons. Spray with Krylon workable fixative.

D   E   F

D Cover the cap with Silver *Krylon* leafing pen.
E Coat the cap with *Triangle Crafts* Sophisticated Finishes Gold Metallic Surfacer.
F Coat the cap with *Triangle Crafts* Sophisticated Finishes Copper Metallic Surfacer.

G   H   I

G Coat the cap with *Triangle Crafts* Sophisticated Finishes Iron Metallic Surfacer.
H Coat the cap with *Triangle Crafts* Sophisticated Finishes Copper Surfacer with Green Patina.
I Coat the cap with *Triangle Crafts* Sophisticated Finishes Gold Surfacer with Blue Patina.

J   K   L

J Coat the cap with *Triangle Crafts* Sophisticated Finishes Iron Surfacer with Rust Patina.
K Coat the cap with *Jacquard* Pinata alcohol inks, first White, then Sapphire Blue.
L Coat with Silver embossing powder.

All Occasion Jewelry

Pins are the most versatile form of jewelry. They can make a statement, express a sentiment, or be purely decorative. Enjoy designing your own custom pieces.

Pins as Jewelry

by Linda Rael

MATERIALS:
Design Originals (Bottle Caps: 1 Gold, 1 Yellow; Stickers: #0668 Fun and Games, #0669 Vintage Children) • Watch parts • 1 head pin • Charms • Beads • Pin backs • Small nail • Hammer • Pliers • *JudiKins* Diamond Glaze • E6000

INSTRUCTIONS:
Place a sticker in the cap, or glue a small image with white glue.
No dangles: Trim the rim of the cap with glitter glue or beads as shown on page 29 for beading the flange of a cap.
Dangles: If you are adding dangles, punch a small hole at the bottom of the bottle cap. Thread a head pin through the hole. Repeat for each dangle.
Glaze image: Pour Diamond Glaze into the cap and allow to dry. If desired, add small watch parts or glitter before the Diamond Glaze is dry.
Add a charm or bead onto the head pin. Wrap head pin wire around itself to secure.
Finish: Glue a pin to the back of the bottle cap with E6000.

Making the Dangles

Use heavy duty jump rings.

  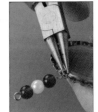 

1. Open a jump ring by twisting it open *'side to side'* using two pair of pliers.

2. Slide a jump ring through a hole in a bottle cap.

3. Slip an eye pin with a loop on the jump ring.

4. Close eye pin securely with pliers.

Little bits of art are a valuable way to practice techniques. Enjoy making this tag.

Bingo Tag

Carrie Edelmann Avery

MATERIALS:
Design Originals (Bottle Cap; #0669 Vintage Children Sticker; #0542 Father's Farm paper) • Gray cardstock • *EK Success* lace • *JudiKins* Diamond Glaze

INSTRUCTIONS:
Cut Gray cardstock 2½" x 3½". Cut Bingo image from Father's Farm paper 2" x 3". Adhere Bingo image and lace to the Gray tag. Flatten a cap. Adhere sticker. Seal the sticker with Diamond Glaze. Let dry. Adhere cap to tag.

Old library cards are great for journaling.

Is something hiding in this pocket?

Yes! It's Dad's old school photo!

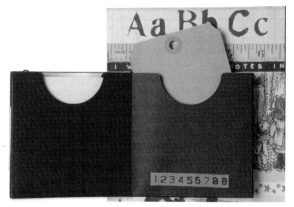

Think of this tag as a canvas just waiting for your art.

Folios and Books

Creativity adds a special touch to cards, gifts and folio mailers. Unity is most appealing when all the components work in harmony to create the desired mood. This folio is a good example of a unique mailable gift. Stickers, travel-theme papers and labels capture that popular vintage look.

European Travel Folio
by Carol Wingert

MATERIALS:
Design Originals (3 Gold Bottle Caps; #0669 Vintage Children Stickers; #0679 Vintage paper) • *Envelopments* folio • Vintage postcards • Movie film • *7gypsies* (Paris clock, waxed linen) • Button • Travel labels (*Cavallini Papers, NRN Designs*) • E6000

INSTRUCTIONS:
Apply paper to the face of the folio.
Add vintage postcard, travel labels, and film.
Apply stickers and clock face to the top of the bottle caps.
Adhere to folio with E6000.
Add button. Wrap the folio with waxed linen to close.

"I will not pass notes in class." Save your school memories, including photos of your friends in this altered coin booklet. The mini book inside is full of envelopes to hold all those forbidden "secret notes".

Coin Booklet

by Renée Plains

MATERIALS:
Design Originals (12 Gold Bottle Caps; #0496 Teadye Alphabet paper) • *Making Memories* (Mini Pocket Book, label holder, Silver brads) • Decorative paper • Half-Dollar coin collecting folder • Muslin strips (2½" x 10"; 2½" x 7⅝") • Cardboard (2 strips ¾" x 7⅝"; 2 pieces 5¾" x 7¾") • Rubber stamps • Ink • Black acrylic paint • Craft knife • 1" circle punch • *SOBO* glue • *JudiKins* Diamond Glaze

INSTRUCTIONS:
Book: Remove 2 coin collecting cards from the folder. • Stack and glue the cardboard strips together. • Lay the coin cards with the cardboard between them leaving ¼" between each piece.
Paint SOBO glue on the longer muslin strip. Place the strip over the boards to bind them together, wrapping the ends towards the inside. Glue the shorter muslin strip on the inside center overlapping the ends of the first piece.
Paint the binding Black. • Cover the inside boards with decorative paper. • Turn the board over so you can see the holes. Cut coin openings with a craft knife on right page.
Cover 2 pieces of cardboard 5¾" x 7¾" with decorative paper for front and back covers. Glue covered cardboard over the outside of holders.
Punch 12 circles from photographs and glue into 12 bottle caps. Place a thin layer of Diamond Glaze in each bottle cap. Let dry.
Glue a bottle cap in each of the openings on the right side of the book.
Mini book: Glue Teadye Alphabet paper to the cover of a Mini Pocket Book. Attach a label holder to the cover with small brads.
Cover the inside front with scrapbook paper. • Stamp pocket pages using your book theme. Place tags and memorabilia in the pockets. Glue the mini book to inside left cover.

Making the Coin Booklet

1. Tear out coin holder section from folder.

2. Place boards and cardboard strip on muslin.

3. Fold the muslin strip to the inside and glue in place.

4. Cut out openings with a craft knife.

5. Glue paper to mini book.

6. Glue mini-book into the project.

Here is a terrific way to display copies of those old time photos and treasures.

The supporting cast of the card are a bit of lace, an old postcard, ribbon, buttons and of course a bottle cap with sticker.

Pretty Face Card
by Judy Claxton

MATERIALS:

Design Originals (Gold Bottle Cap; #0664 School Days Sticker) • Navy Blue cardstock • Decorative paper (Blue paisley, Postcard, Ivory) • Transparency from a photo • Gold photo corners • Light Blue buttons • Dark Blue ribbon • Lace • *Stampington* rubber stamps (Recommendation, Post Cube) • Fine line Gold embossing powder • *ColorBox* inkpads (Metalextra Gold Rush, Creamy Beige Fluid Chalk) • *Posh Rainbow* Blue Metallic ink • Sponge • Heat gun • *Tombow* glue stick • *Crafter's Pick* The Ultimate! glue

INSTRUCTIONS:

Card: Cut Navy cardstock 6½" x 11". Fold to 5½" x 6½".

Mat: Use both stamps and Gold ink to decorate the Blue Paisley paper. Emboss the images with Gold fine line embossing powder. Glue the mat in place.

Collage: Cut out postcard. Sponge edges with Creamy Beige. Glue lace, postcard, ribbon, and buttons to card. • Attach transparency to Ivory paper. Add photo corners. Adhere to card.

Accents: Color cap with Metallic Blue ink. Adhere the sticker and a small button to the cap. Glue the cap in place.

This artistic collage is the perfect presentation for travel memorabilia... it helps keep the memory alive.

Evening in Paris Shoes
by Judy Claxton

MATERIALS:

Design Originals: (Black Bottle Cap, #0669 Vintage Children Sticker; #0529 Le Jardin paper) • Black cardstock • Decorative papers (Lime, Black) • Black eyelets • *Meri Meri Accents* Fancy shoes • *USArtQuest* Small Mica Chip • Plastic clock numerals • *Stampington* stamps (Blooming Bold, The Kiss) • Ink (*ColorBox* Metalextra Gold Rush; *Tsukineko* Staz-On Black) • Red Liner tape • *Crafter's Pick* The Ultimate! glue

INSTRUCTIONS:

Card: Cut Black cardstock 7½" x 10". Fold to 5" x 7½". Stamp the Blooming Bold image with Gold.

Mats: Cut: Lime 4½" x 7"; Black 4¼" x 6¾". • Adhere mats to card.

Accents: Stamp 'The Kiss' image on the mica with Black. • Tear a row of ladies from Le Jardin paper and glue it to the card. • Apply the sticker to the cap. • Tape the fancy shoes and cap to the card. • Attach the Mica with 2 eyelets. • Glue the number in place.

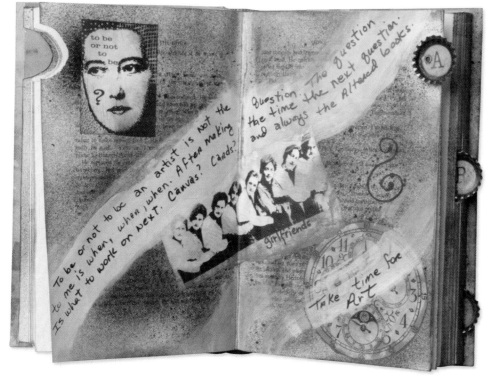

Bottle Cap Tabs in an Altered Book
by Beverly Seymour

MATERIALS:

Design Originals (Bottle Caps; #0673 Typewriter ABC stickers) • Eyelets • Old book to alter • *B-Line Design* Rubber stamps (Time; Classmates; Texture Cube; Musing)

INSTRUCTIONS:

Cut out circular nesting areas on the edge of the pages in a book. Punch a hole in each bottle cap. Add a sticker. Use eyelets to attach the bottle caps in position as tabs in a book.

A stamped flower and a ring of beads create a complementary embellishment for this simple decorated notebook.

Blue Notebook
by Shari Carroll

MATERIALS:

Design Originals White Bottle Cap • Small notebook • Glossy paper • Small "E" beads • Ribbon • *Hero Arts* (Script, Small flower) • Fine print White embossing powder • Ink (Black, White) • White spray paint • Heat gun • 1" circle punch • E6000 • Glue Dots

INSTRUCTIONS:

Stamp and emboss script in White on notebook. Let dry. • Flatten a cap and spray inside White. Let dry. • Fill the trough with E6000 and beads. • Stamp and color a small flower on glossy paper. Punch out the flower image and adhere it in the cap. • Adhere the cap to the notebook with a large Glue Dot and tie ribbon around the bottom.

Feeling fruity? Well, this is one of the most refreshing cards in the whole book. You can almost smell the citrus. Stir up a pitcher of lemonade and invite your friends over to make these very fruity cards.

Lemon, Lime, and Orange
by Judy Claxton

MATERIALS:
Design Originals (Bottle Caps: Yellow, Orange, Green; #0670 Citrus Brights Stickers) • Cardstock (Beige, Orange, Yellow, Lime Green) • Beige *Magic Mesh* • 3 Tags • Ribbon (Yellow Check, Lime Check, Orange Check) • Eyelets (Yellow, Lime Green, Orange) • *Ink-It* (Orange acrylic paint, Alcohol inks: Yellow, Lime) • *ColorBox* Fluid Chalk Amber Clay • Magazine photos (lemons, limes, oranges) • Computer generated words with Orange ink • Zig-zag scissors (Large, small) • *Crafter's Pick* The Ultimate! glue • *Tombow* glue stick • Red Liner tape

INSTRUCTIONS:
Card: Cut Beige cardstock 6¾" x 8½". Fold to 4¼" x 6¾".
Mats: Cut: Orange 4" x 6¼" with large scissors; Yellow 3½" x 6⅛" with small scissors; Green 3⅜" x 6". • Adhere the mats and mesh to the card.
Tags: Glue images of fruit to tags and trim to fit. • Add matching eyelets and ribbons and tape to the card.
Accents: Use alcohol inks to color the inside of the Yellow cap Yellow, the Green cap Lime. Let dry. Add stickers. • Paint the Orange cap with Orange acrylic paint. Let dry and add stickers. • Glue caps to the card. • Ink the edge of the card.

Password Card

by Kathy Martin

1960's retro meets 21st century text messaging. You'll feel groovy as you make this fun card.

MATERIALS:
Design Originals (Bottle Caps; #1209 Text Messages Stickers) • Cardstock (Glossy Black, White) • Buttons • *Postmodern Design* stamps (Harlequin Diamonds, Gothic Lower Alphabet) • *ColorBox* Chalks (Lime Pastel, Tangerine, Lavender, Rouge) • *Tsukineko* StazOn Black ink • *Houston Arts* Omni Gel • *JudiKins* Diamond Glaze

INSTRUCTIONS:
Card: Cut Black cardstock 8½" x 12". Fold to 6" x 8½".
Mats: Cut: White 5½" x 8½" and apply Chalks direct to paper; Glossy Black 4¼" x 8½". • Glue mats to card.
Words: On White cardstock, stamp Harlequin Diamonds in Lavender and overstamp the alphabet letters in Black. Tear the edges of the word strips so they are 2" wide. Mask the diamonds and apply chalks direct to paper. Glue the words to the card.
Accents: Glue novelty buttons in place. • Partially smash 2 caps. Apply stickers inside the caps and fill with Glaze. Glue the caps to the card with Omni Gel. Let dry overnight.

MATERIALS:
Design Originals #1209 Text Messages stickers • *Paper Reflections* Bags & Cards • *Bazzill* cardstock • Decorative Paper (*Treehouse Designs* Multicolor Dots; *Colorbok* Purple Tiles; *KI Memories* Turquoise stripe; *Making Memories* Black gingham; *Doodlebug Design* Purple Dots, Green Dots; Green plaid) • 1" Metal Rimmed Tags • *Making Memories* (Paper flowers, Metal letters, Ribbon slide) • *EK Success* Punches • Brads • Ribbons • Fibers • Adhesive

INSTRUCTIONS:
Cover the 2¼" x 3¼" card with cardstock and decorative paper. Embellish as desired.
Add sticker to metal rimmed tag. Adhere tag to card.

Q.T. Notes - Quick and Tiny

by Susan Keuter

Make these little notes up in just a few minutes with a variety of scrapbook leftovers. Spend an evening making up a whole stack. Adhere metal rimmed tag, but leave it blank.

Then, when a need arises, choose stickers to convey a message. Use them for all sorts of "I'm thinking of you" situations. Tuck one in your daughter's lunch on the day of the big test. Hide one in your son's backpack before the Championship game. Put one in your husband's briefcase before he leaves for the office. When Grandpa and Grandma are packing to go home, sneak one in their suitcase.

Looking to use up some leftover embellishments? Check out this simple belted notebook cover made with odd bits and pieces.

Belted Journal
by Diana McMillan

MATERIALS:

Design Originals (Navy Blue Bottle Cap; #0676 All American paper; #0664 School Days stickers) • 7½" x 9¾" notebook • Metal pieces (buckle, letters, gear, swirl, Yellow and Green 1" circle brads, 3 stars) • Wood game piece • 1 pair google eyes • Red ribbon 1½" wide • E6000 • *Therm O Web* Memory Tape Runner

INSTRUCTIONS:

Book: Cover the front and back of the notebook with All American paper using Memory Tape Runner. • Cut enough ribbon to wrap from the inside front cover, across the front and back and around to the inside of the back cover. Glue the ribbon in place with E6000.

Accents: Flatten a cap. Apply the sticker. Adhere decorations to the book with E6000.

Citrus gives this notebook a twist with its unique closure. Don't miss this cool technique.

Twist Journal
by pj dutton

MATERIALS:

Design Originals (2 Orange Bottle Caps; #0670 Citrus Brights Stickers; #0680 Citrus paper) • 7½" x 9¾" notebook • 2 Gold eyelets • 18" Black waxed linen • *Xyron* adhesive

INSTRUCTIONS:

Front cover: Cut Citrus paper 6¾" x 9½". Run through Xyron and adhere to notebook cover, starting at Black spine and leaving ⅛" border at top, bottom, and open edge of book.

Back cover: Cut Citrus paper 5¼" x 9¾". Run through Xyron. Score lines referring to diagrams. Fold paper on the 1⅜" score, adhering it to itself. Adhere

right edge to book. Fold doubled flap around to the front.

Closure: Place stickers in 2 caps. Flatten caps. Punch hole in middle of each cap. Position cap on book; set an eyelet in each cap. Tie waxed linen around outer cap; wrap it around cap on the front cover.

1. With sticker in place, crimp edges of cap down.

2. Set the eyelet through bottle cap and journal cover.

Twist Journal Diagrams

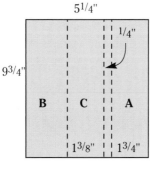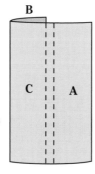

1. Cut decorative paper and fold along dashed lines.

5¼"

¼"

9¾"

B   C   A

1⅜"   1¾"

2. Glue A to journal back cover. Fold B over journal edge and glue to C. The ¼" space allows for journal pages.

B

C   A

This is a great beginner project. It's easy and inexpensive because you make your own paper beads!

Bookmark

by Lynn Krucke

MATERIALS:

Design Originals (Bottle Caps; #0670 Citrus Brights Stickers; #0680 Citrus papers) • ³⁄₈" wide Avocado Green grosgrain ribbon • 28" Green waxed linen thread • *Artistic Wire* 22 gauge Tangerine • Assorted small glass beads • Large bead with a hole large enough for ribbon to pass through • Wire cutters • Small paintbrush • Toothpicks • *JudiKins* Diamond Glaze

INSTRUCTIONS:

Bottle Caps: Flatten caps. Make a small hole at top of each cap. • Adhere stickers to caps. Coat stickers with Diamond Glaze. Let dry.

Rolled beads: Use pattern to cut out triangles. Discard right triangles at each end. • With colored side of paper face down, roll a triangle of paper around a toothpick from the wide edge to its point. Smear a little Diamond Glaze on paper after you get the wrap started to glue it together. Be careful not to glue bead to toothpick. Allow beads to dry. Brush on 1-2 coats of Diamond Glaze to strengthen them.

Ribbon: Cut a 14" length. To prevent fraying, coat cut ends lightly with Diamond Glaze. Let dry. • Slide a large bead on 1 end and tie knot to secure it. • Fold cut edge of ribbon over knot, tightly wrap wire around it to secure. Trim wire ends.

Fringe: Cut three 7" pieces of thread. Holding them together, tie a knot near one end, pull tight. • Tie knot at other end of ribbon, but push bundle of thread through middle of knot before tightening it. Fold cut edge of ribbon over knot, wrap with wire as before. • Thread glass and paper beads onto each piece of thread as desired. Tie a completed cap onto end of each strand.

Bead Patterns

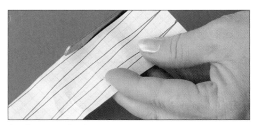

1. Cut on the lines.

2. Starting with wide end, roll paper on a toothpick.

Use those negative stencils to embellish your card. Make a special "thinking of you" card with an initial. The bottle cap is spray painted to match.

"P" Art Card

by Shari Carroll

MATERIALS:

Bazzill cardstock (Sherbet, Pear, White) • Decorative paper • Eiffel Tower charm • Ribbon • 1 jump ring • *Hero Arts* "Art" stamp • Black ink • Pear spray paint • Nail • Hammer • 1" circle punch • Adhesive

INSTRUCTIONS:

Card: Cut White cardstock 6" x 8". Fold to 4" x 6". Cut a Pear mat 3½" x 5½" Tear the bottom of the mat and adhere to the card. • Cut a Sherbet mat 3¼" x 5¼". Tear the bottom of the mat and adhere to the card.

Accents: Cut an initial from the decorative paper and sand the edges to age. Add the ribbon. Glue the initial to the card. • Flatten a bottle cap with a mallet. Punch a hole in the bottom edge. Paint the cap. Allow to dry. • Attach a jump ring with charm. • Stamp "Art" on decorative paper and punch it out. Glue the circle to the bottle cap. Adhere the cap to the card.

Add some drama to your fashion statement with bold colorful earrings. You will love the dangles.

Earrings
by Gail Ellspermann

MATERIALS:

Design Originals (2 Black Bottle Caps; #0670 Citrus Brights Stickers) • Orange E-beads • Earring findings • 8 Silver jump rings • 6 head pins • *JudiKins* Diamond Glaze

INSTRUCTIONS:

Cap: Punch holes in each top and bottom of caps. Insert a jump ring in each hole. • Add stickers. Apply a line of Glaze to inside edge of cap. Place beads in Glaze. Make sure jump rings are straight as Glaze dries. Let dry overnight.

Dangles: See dangle diagrams. Attach dangles to earring with a jump ring. Attach earring wires to the top of the cap with jump rings.

1. Thread 11 beads on head pin. Make curl in end with needle-nose pliers. Make 3 dangles for each earring.

2. Bend dangle as shown. Thread dangles on jump ring. Close jump ring.

Give your next party a special touch with individual place cards. Guests can take them home.

Place Card
by Molly Jennings

MATERIALS:

Design Originals (Silver Bottle Cap; #1211 Fun Faces Stickers) • White cardstock • Orange origami paper • Red sequin • *VersaColor* Orange ink pad • Fine point black marker • Pencil with new eraser • GOOP glue

INSTRUCTIONS:

Cut White cardstock 4¼" x 5". Fold to 2½" x 4¼". Cut origami paper 1¾" x 2¼" and fold into a hat following the steps below. Using pencil eraser, stamp 6 small Orange circles across the bottom of place card. Brush folded edge of card with Orange inkpad. Cut ¾" strip of White cardstock, write name with marker, then cut to fit. Edge strip with Orange inkpad Flatten a cap. Apply the sticker. Place the hat on the cap. Glue a sequin to the hat. Glue the cap to the card.

1. Fold 1¾" x 2¼" paper in half (solid color on outside).

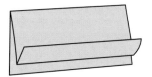

2. Fold up edge ³⁄₁₆". Turn paper over.

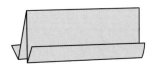

3. Repeat step 2 and unfold both edges.

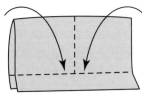

4. Fold each corner down to center and bottom fold.

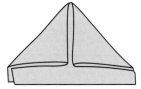

5. Your paper will look like this.

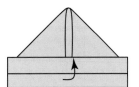

6. Turn up edge again. Turn over.

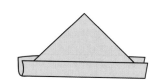

7. Repeat step 6. Turn over.

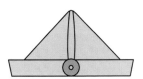

8. Glue a sequin to hat front.

Beep, Beep! Stop here for a fun idea! Bottle caps form a traffic light.

Way to Go! Card   *by Susan Keuter*

MATERIALS:
Design Originals Bottle Caps • *Bazzill* cardstock (Red, Yellow, Black, Green) • *Making Memories* Black Gingham paper • *Creative Imaginations* Sticker Letters • *twopeasinabucket.com* Flea Market Computer Font • *Deluxe Designs* Card Template 9-C

INSTRUCTIONS:
Words: Print journaling to fit on a Green 2¼" square. Cut out the journal box.
Card: Cut Red cardstock 7" x 10". Fold in half to 5" x 7".
Mats: Cut: Black 1¾" x 4" and 2⅜" x 3"; 4 Check 1¼" x 1¼"; Yellow 1¼" x 2⅝" and ⅝" x 2⅜". • Adhere the mats to the card as in the photo.
Finish: Add stickers. Glue caps in place.

Next time a friend needs a lift, make this quick Smile card to raise their spirits!

Smile Card   *by Carrie Edelmann Avery*

MATERIALS:
Design Originals (Bottle Caps; #0670 Brights Stickers) • Cardstock (Red, Silver) • *Tsukineko* StazOn Black ink • Rubber Stamps (*Hero Arts* Alphabet, Swirl; *Making Memories* Alphabet) • Red ink • Foam dots

INSTRUCTIONS:
Cut Red cardstock 8" x 8¼". Fold to 4" x 8¼". Stamp with Red swirls. • Cut a Silver mat 2¼" x 8¼". Adhere to card. Stamp words "you make me" with Black. • Stamp stickers with Black ink. Apply stickers to caps. Attach caps to card with foam dots.

Fun Cards To Give

Why spend a fortune buying a gift bag when you can make this one to coordinate with your gift?

This gift bag uses a fabulous new technique with glossy white cardstock and chalk inks. The design possibilities are nearly limitless.

Gift Bag Gusset Pattern

Gusset Diagram
Cut 2 and fold along dashed lines. Glue to the inside ends of Gift Bag.

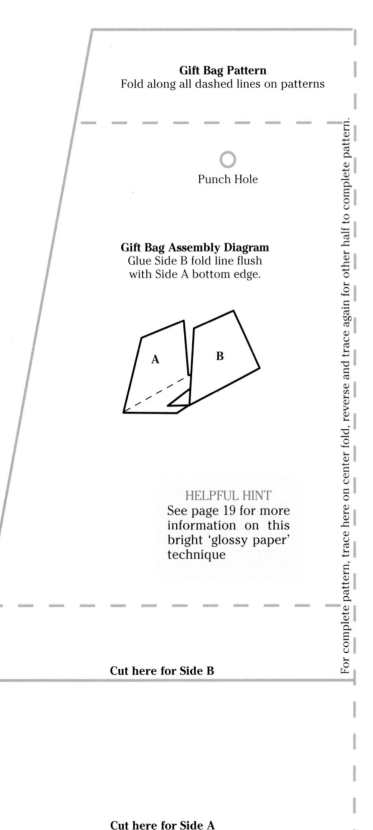

Gift Bag Pattern
Fold along all dashed lines on patterns

○
Punch Hole

Gift Bag Assembly Diagram
Glue Side B fold line flush with Side A bottom edge.

A   B

HELPFUL HINT
See page 19 for more information on this bright 'glossy paper' technique

For complete pattern, trace here on center fold, reverse and trace again for other half to complete pattern.

Cut here for Side B

Cut here for Side A

1. Smoosh the Yellow pad onto glossy cardstock then stamp all Yellow images. Let dry. Wipe off chalky residue.

2. Continue the pattern with Olive pad and stamp Olive images. Let dry and wipe off chalky residue.

3. The Olive is supposed to smear more than Yellow.
Add Burnt Sienna sparingly in the same manner.

Sunshine Gift Bag

by Kathy Martin

MATERIALS:

Design Originals (Black Bottle Caps; #0664 School stickers) • 2 sheets Glossy White cardstock • Black cording for handle • Copper eyelets • *Postmodern Design* da Vinci Shapes Cube stamp • *ColorBox* Chalks (Yellow Ochre, Olive Green, Burnt Sienna) • *JudiKins* Diamond Glaze • *Houston Arts* Omni Gel • Red Liner tape • Eyelet tools • Ruler • Bone folder • Pencil • Scissors • Facial tissue

INSTRUCTIONS:

Tip: This project uses Yellow Ochre, Olive Pastel and Burnt Sienna because those colors work the best to create a wonderful 3-dimensional look and a beautiful blend of colors.

Paper: Smoosh the Yellow pad onto the Glossy White cardstock in a geometric pattern, like loose bricks. Stamp all Yellow images. Let dry completely. Use a tissue to buff off the chalky residue. • Continue the brick pattern with Olive and stamp Olive images. When the ink is partially dry, use a tissue to buff residue off the paper. The Olive is supposed to smear much more than the Yellow. • Use Burnt Sienna sparingly. Dab a little and smear. Add finer detail stamp images. To keep the finer detail intact, allow the ink to totally dry before you buff.

Bag: Use the template to trace the shapes on the back of your paper. There are 2 large pieces for the front and back. The "side" pattern must be cut out twice. Use ruler and bone folder to create crease lines where indicated on template.

Assembly: Place tape along the folded edges of the two side pieces. The top edge folds down onto itself so tape it on the inside. All other folds tape on the outside. • Place tape along the inside top flap of the front and back panels and seal folded. • Set 2 eyelets on each side of the bag. • Place tape on the short bottom flap of the back panel, and press back and front panels together. Tape the 2 side panels to this piece to form a cross. • Tape a side panel to the main purse starting at the bottom tab and working up to the top of the purse. Repeat for the other side. Align the edges. Adjust the side panels and then tape down the top flaps of the side panels.

Handle: Add cording.

Use stickers and bottle caps to embellish the flower centers on your card for an added bit of color and dimension.

Flower Card

by Sally Traidman

MATERIALS:

Design Originals (3 Bottle Caps; #0670 Citrus Brights Stickers; #0549 Shorthand paper) • Cardstock (Cream, Fuschia, Orange, Yellow, Green) • Adhesive

INSTRUCTIONS:

Card: Cut the Cream cardstock 6" x 8½". Fold to 4¼" x 6". Cut a Shorthand mat 3¾" x 5¼". Adhere mat to card.

Accents: Cut out flowers and leaves. • Flatten 3 caps. Add stickers. Adhere flowers, leaves and stickers to the card.

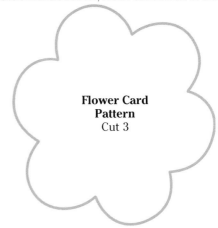

**Flower Card Pattern
Cut 3**

Art Can Be Fun

MATERIALS:

Design Originals (2 Gold Bottle Caps; #0670 Citrus Brights Stickers) • Cardstock (Glossy Black, White) • *Postmodern Design* stamps (Fancy Diamond Cube, Words in Diamonds, Three Rows, Gothic Lower alphabet) • *ColorBox* Chalks (Lime Pastel, Peach Pastel, Lavender, Rouge) • *Tsukineko* StazOn Black ink • *Houston Arts* Omni Gel • *JudiKins* Diamond Glaze

INSTRUCTIONS:

Card: Cut Black cardstock 8½" x 11". Fold to 5½" x 8½". **Mats**: Cut: Glossy Black 3¼" x 8½"; White 7¾" x 8½". • On White mat, stamp large diamond shape in random pattern using Lime Pastel and Rouge. Overstamp using smaller diamond shape and words in diamonds so that images are slightly offset from larger diamonds. • Cut stamped paper into two 8½" pieces, 5" wide and 2½" wide. **Small mat**: Apply Chalks direct to paper. Stamp more small diamonds with Peach Pastel. **Accents**: Glue mats to card. • Stamp phrase "art can be fun". • Place stickers inside 2 caps and fill with Glaze. Glue to card with Omni Gel. Let dry overnight.

Love Joy

MATERIALS:

Design Originals (3 Gold Bottle Caps; #0669 Vintage Children Stickers) • Cardstock (Glossy Black, White) • *Postmodern Design* Large Block of Words stamp • *ColorBox* Chalks (Lime Pastel, Wisteria, Rouge) • *Marvy* Yellow-Green Matchables ink • Facial tissue • *Houston Arts* Omni Gel • *JudiKins* Diamond Glaze

INSTRUCTIONS:

Card: Cut Black cardstock 8½" x 10". Fold to 5" x 8½". **Mats**: Cut: Glossy Black 1¾" x 8½"; Glossy White 5" x 8½". Stain White mat with Lime Pastel and Wisteria applied direct to paper. Quickly smear colors using clean tissue. Buff paper to remove ink residue. • Stamp words twice with Rouge. Quickly smear image with clean tissue. (The Red color sinks quickly into paper and does not smear much). • Repeat using Lime Pastel, but allow the Green to dry thoroughly before buffing with clean tissue. (It takes longer for the Green to stain the paper.) • Fill in "White" spaces by smearing Marvy Yellow-Green ink direct to paper and quickly buffing with clean tissue. • Cut a ⅜" x 8½" strip off stained mat. Adhere mats to card placing strip down middle.

Accents: Apply stickers inside 3 caps. Fill caps with Glaze. Glue the caps to the card with Omni Gel. Let dry overnight.

Oh Happy Day

MATERIALS:
Design Originals (3 Gold Bottle Caps; Stickers: #0664 School Days, #0669 Vintage Children) • Glossy Cardstock (Black, White) • *Postmodern Design* da Vinci Shapes Cube stamp • *ColorBox* Chalks (Wisteria, Warm Red, Creamy Brown) • *Marvy* Matchables Yellow-Green ink • Cotton swab • *Houston Arts* Omni Gel • *JudiKins* Diamond Glaze

INSTRUCTIONS:
Card: Cut Black cardstock 6" x 9". Fold to 4½" x 6".
Mats: Cut White cardstock 4¼" x 5¾". Stamp circle images repeatedly using Chalks. Use a cotton swab to stain the paper around the circles with Yellow-Green ink. • Glue the mat to the card.
Accents: Place stickers inside caps and fill with Glaze. Glue caps to the card with Omni Gel. Let dry overnight.

Memories

MATERIALS:
Design Originals (Gold Bottle Cap; #0669 Vintage Children Stickers) • Cardstock (Glossy Black, White) • *Postmodern Design* (Clear Cuts #18; Rubber stamps: Retro Pattern Cube, Mexican Image Cube) • *ColorBox* Chalks (Lime Pastel, Wisteria, Warm Red, Creamy Brown) • *Marvy* Matchables inks (Caribbean Blue, Yellow-Green) • *Gary Burlin* Square brads • Facial tissue • *Houston Arts* Omni Gel • *JudiKins* Diamond Glaze

INSTRUCTIONS:
Card: Cut Black cardstock 6" x 12". Fold to 6" x 6".
Mats: Cut: Glossy Black 3½" x 3½"; Glossy White 5½" x 5½" and 3" x 3".
Large Mat: Stamp the Mexican Image with Wisteria and Lime Pastel. When partially dry, buff the surface with a clean tissue. Some smearing should occur. • Fill in the "White" spaces with Caribbean Blue ink direct to paper. Quickly smear with a clean tissue.
Small mat: Stamp the Retro Pattern with Warm Red, Wisteria, and Creamy Brown. When partially dry, buff surface with a tissue. • Fill in the "White" spaces with Yellow-Green ink direct to paper. Quickly smear with a tissue.
Assembly: Adhere mats to the card. Add brads. • Adhere transparency to card.
Accents: Place a sticker inside a cap and fill with Glaze. Glue the cap to the card with Omni Gel. Let dry overnight.

Smear Inks

Special Technique
by Kathy Martin

White glossy paper is made with a clay finish. Clay minerals are negatively charged.

Inks are made with pigments that are actually minerals that can be positively or negatively charged. If you think back to chemistry class, you remember that "opposites attract" and "likes repel like".

Chalks have positively charged minerals that will be strongly attracted to paper and sink in very deeply.

The negatively charged minerals in chalks will be repelled by the clay on the paper.

Use 3 colors with varying degrees of positive charge (strong, medium and weak). So not only are the colors attracted to the paper, they actually repel each other when you layer color on top of color. This chemical reaction is what allows you to make an eye-boggling 3-dimensional effect with hardly any effort at all.

Bold images with lots of White space work best with this technique.

Fine line images may or may not show up as vibrantly, but certainly can be used to add texture and interest to the final piece.

I opened
the doors
of my heart
and behold
there was
music within
and a song.

Jean Ingelow

Using Kathy Martin's foolproof technique for stamping on transparencies, you can make elegant cards with simple materials.

Elegant Cards
by Kathy Martin

GENERAL MATERIALS:
Marvy Matchables Ochre • Clear transparency film • *Tsukineko* Black StazOn ink • *Houston Arts* Omni Gel • *JudiKins* Diamond Glaze • Xyron adhesive

GENERAL INSTRUCTIONS:
For stamping on transparency film, see steps below. "Lets Decorate". After transparency is dry, run it through a Xyron, then adhere it to card.

Rose Card
MATERIALS:
Design Originals Bottle Cap • *Postmodern Design* rubber stamps (Fancy Square Cube, Large Rose Panel) • Cardstock (Glossy Black, Green, Tan, Ivory)

INSTRUCTIONS:
Card: Cut Black cardstock 7" x 9". Fold to 4½" x 7". • **Mats**: Cut a Green mat 4¼" x 7". Stamp the Fancy Square along edges of the Green mat with Black ink. • Cut a Black mat 3¼" x 7". • Cut a Tan mat 3" x 7". Adhere the mats to the card. • **Focal point**: Cut an Ivory mat 2¼" x 7". Ink the edges with Ochre. Stamp Rose Panel on a clear transparency, adhere it to card. **Accent**: Partially smash a bottle cap. Place an image inside the cap and fill with Diamond Glaze. Glue the bottle cap to the card with Omni Gel and allow to dry overnight.

Joy Card
MATERIALS:
Design Originals (3 Black Bottle Caps; #0672 Walnut Alphabet Stickers) • *Postmodern Design* rubber stamps (Leaf & Berry Corner, Swirls & Dots Corner) • Cardstock (Glossy Black, Tan)

INSTRUCTIONS:
Card: Cut Black cardstock 8½" x 9". Fold to 4½" x 8½". • Cut a Tan mat 4" x 8½". Stamp the transparency. Cut each square design on the diagonal. Adhere it to the card. • **Accent**: Partially smash 3 bottle caps. Place a sticker inside each cap and coat with Diamond Glaze. Let dry. Glue the bottle caps to the card with Omni Gel and allow to dry overnight.

Burgundy Card
MATERIALS:
Design Originals Silver Bottle Cap • *Postmodern Design* rubber stamps (Leaf & Berry Bar, A Loving Heart quote) • Cardstock (Glossy Black, Burgundy) • *Jacquard* Pearl Ex powders

INSTRUCTIONS:
Card: Cut Black cardstock 6" x 10½". Fold to 5¼" x 6". • Cut a Burgundy mat 4¾" x 6". Adhere the mat to the card. • Stamp the transparency. Cut out the design. Color the back of the transparency with Pearl Ex and adhere it to the card. • **Accent**: Partially smash a bottle cap. Place an image inside the cap and coat with Diamond Glaze. Let dry. Adhere the bottle cap to the card with a foam dot. • Stamp the quote on the card.

Transferring with Transparency Film

1. Lay transparency film over inked stamp.

2. Press with a finger until the design is transferred.

Tip: This transparency technique also works well with vellum and glass slides. Be sure to let the StazOn dry completely.

Elegant Beauty

This ornament could easily convert to a tag embellishment on a card, photo frame, or gift basket by adding your artistic expression.

Yesteryear Ornament Tag
by Amy Wellenstein

MATERIALS:
Design Originals (Black Bottle Cap; #0669 Vintage Children Stickers) • Matboard • *Making Memories* eyelet • *May Arts* ribbon • *Dymo* Label (maker, tape) • Eyelet tools • ⅛" punch • Cosmetic sponge • *Stampotique Originals* rubber stamps (Antique Border, Joy definition) • Ink (*Tsukineko* Versafine pigment: Onyx Black; *Ranger* Adirondack dye: Sepia, Maroon) • *Sakura* Hobby Crafts Crystal Lacquer • *Crafter's Pick* The Ultimate! Glue

INSTRUCTIONS:
Trim matboard into a house-shaped ornament. • Sponge Maroon and Sepia inks on the ornament. • Stamp 'Antique Border' across the bottom of the ornament using Onyx Black ink. Stamp 'Joy definition' in the center using the same ink. • Set an eyelet at the top of the ornament. • Adhere a sticker inside the bottle cap. Fill the bottle cap half full with Crystal Lacquer. Let dry. • Glue bottle cap to the center of the ornament. • Create the words MERRY CHRISTMAS with a label maker. Adhere below the bottle cap. • Tie a ribbon through the eyelet.

1. Sponge the inks on the ornament.

2. Stamp the ornament.

3. Punch a hole for the ribbon.

Bottle Cap Journal

by Renée Plains

MATERIALS:
Design Originals 9 Gold Bottle Caps • Purchased journal • Decorative paper • 1" circle punch • *JudiKins* Diamond Glaze • E6000

INSTRUCTIONS:
Cut paper slightly smaller than the journal and glue it to the journal cover.
Punch 9 photos from a photocopy. • Adhere punched photos in bottle caps. Cover photos with a thin layer of Diamond Glaze. Let dry.
Position bottle caps on journal cover; glue in place.

Magical Memories

Tags will always be a favorite art form because they are so versatile. Use them as embellishments or as stand-alone artistic expressions. Either way, you will enjoy making these creative pieces.

Wonder Tag
by Carrie Edelmann Avery

MATERIALS:
Design Originals Black Bottle Cap • Black cardstock • Decorative Burgundy paper • *Eclectic Omnibus* image • "wonder" Rub-On • Fibers • 1" circle punch • *JudiKins* Diamond Glaze

INSTRUCTIONS:
Mount Burgundy paper to a Black tag. • Flatten a bottle cap. Punch out the image and adhere it to the cap. Cover the image with Diamond Glaze. Let dry. • Add fibers and Rub-On.

Discover Tag
by Carrie Edelmann Avery

MATERIALS:
Design Originals Silver Bottle Cap • Burgundy cardstock • *Eclectic Omnibus* image • *Making Memories* rubber stamp • *Pebbles, Inc.* "discover" sticker • Fibers • Acrylic paint • 1" circle punch • *JudiKins* Diamond Glaze

INSTRUCTIONS:
Randomly apply acrylic paint to the cardstock. Let dry. • Stamp a pattern across the painted surface, building up layers of color, texture, and pattern. • Punch out the image and adhere it inside the bottle cap. Fill the cap with Diamond Glaze. Let dry. • Add fibers and "discover" sticker.

Look at all the different textures in this peaceful "Thinking of You" card. The decorative paper has gold script. The canvas and ribbon add a woven fabric feel. The flattened bottle cap gives a metallic, bumpy look.

Peace Card
by Carol Wingert

MATERIALS:

Design Originals (Gold Bottle Cap; #0669 Vintage Children Stickers; #5209 Masterpieces in Clay transfer image p. 26) • Cardstock (7" x 10½" Cream, 4¾" x 6½" Burgundy) • 3¾" x 4½" canvas • *7gypsies* paper • *Memory Lane* twill • *Krylon* Gold leafing pen • *Golden* gel medium • *Liquitex* Brown gesso • Brayer • Wet sponge • Sandpaper • E6000

INSTRUCTIONS:

Gel transfer: Paint gel medium on the canvas where the image will be placed. Place a color photo copy of the image face down onto the gel. Burnish or brayer well. Allow to dry overnight. Moisten paper with a wet sponge and gently rub off the paper until the image is clear.

Bottle cap: Flatten a bottle cap. Lightly sand "Peace" sticker, then dry brush with Brown gesso

Card: Fold card to 5¼" x 7". Trim the card edge with Gold leafing. • Adhere Burgundy cardstock, paper, and canvas. Adhere the ribbon and bottle cap to the card with E6000.

There are many ways to transfer images! If you haven't tried this technique, it is worth learning. It allows you to apply images to a variety of surfaces with little expense.

Wild Wild West Card
by Carol Wingert

MATERIALS:

Design Originals (Gold Bottle Cap; #0667 Walnut Numbers Stickers; #5209 Masterpieces in Clay transfer image p. 27) • *Basic Grey* paper • 7" x 11" Burgundy cardstock • Leather button • *7gypsies* (Printed twill, Color wash) • 4" x 5" Craft wood • *Memory Lane* waxed cotton • *Elmers* caulk • *Liquitex* Brown gesso • Brayer or spoon • Wet sponge

INSTRUCTIONS:

Caulk transfer: Paint the surface of the wood with caulk where the image will be placed.

• Lay a color photocopy of the image face down on the caulk and brayer or burnish with a spoon. Let dry overnight.

To remove paper, rub with a wet sponge until the paper begins to soften. Gently rub with a thumb until the paper is gone. Allow to dry. • Adhere waxed cotton and a bottle cap accent to a corner with E6000.

Card: Fold card to 5½" x 7". Adhere paper to the card front. Apply Brown gesso around the edges of the card. Let dry. • Adhere the wood, ribbon, and button to the card with E6000.

Time has been transformed into a stunning silver pendant doll. This "Dream Girl" has all the time in the world. I hope you take the time to enjoy this project.

Dream Girl Pendant   *by Mary Kaye Seckler*

MATERIALS:

Design Originals (Bottle Cap; #1212 Art Elements sticker) • Charms (face, hands, feet) • 1 Silver button with shank removed • 6 Silver jump rings • 1 eye pin • Ball chain with clasp • *Coffee Break Designs* 8 Black open balls • $1/16$" hole punch • Jewelry pliers (round & flat nose) • Wire cutters • *JudiKins* Diamond Glaze

INSTRUCTIONS:

Flatten a bottle cap. • Insert an eye pin through the top of the face charm. Bend eye pin at a 90° angle. Shorten the eye pin to $3/8$". Use round-nosed pliers to make a loop below the face.
• Punch 5 holes in the edge of the bottle cap in the following order: punch a hole at the top for the head; skip 5 spaces and punch a hole for the arm; skip 3 spaces and punch 2 holes in a row for the legs; skip 3 spaces and punch a hole for the arm.
• Attach charms to the bottle cap with jump rings. • Add a jump ring to the top loop of the eye pin and run a piece of ball chain through the loop. Attach Black open balls at random on the ball chain. This adds decoration to the chain while keeping the clasp from traveling from the back of your neck. • Add the Silver button to the front of the bottle cap with a Glue Dot. Adhere the clock sticker to the back of the cap. Coat the sticker with Diamond Glaze so the pendant wears well.

Fun with Bottle Caps

Less is more. Sometimes a simple initial says it all. Make this card for a simple 'thinking of you'.

'S' Card   *by Sally Traidman*

MATERIALS:

Design Originals (Silver Bottle Cap; #0673 Typewriter Alphabet Stickers) • Cardstock (Ivory, Tan, Black) • Dot ribbon • Red Liner tape

INSTRUCTIONS:

Card: Cut Ivory cardstock $5^1/2$" x $8^1/2$". Fold to $4^1/4$" x $5^1/2$". • Cut a Black mat $2^1/4$" x $2^3/4$". Cut a Tan mat 2" x $2^1/2$". • Wrap the mats with the ribbon. Adhere the mats to the card.
• **Accent:** Flatten the cap and affix letter sticker. Tape the cap to the card.

Capture the romance of travel with this collage.

Spain Card   *by Sally Traidman*

MATERIALS:

Design Originals (Bottle Caps: 1 Gold, 1 Silver; #0673 Typewriter Alphabet Stickers; Papers: #0549 Shorthand, #0553) • Black cardstock • 2" paper scraps (Corrugated, Tan, Blue, Green) • 2 round metal rimmed tags • *Hero Arts* Alphabet stamps • Black ink • Circle punch ($1^1/4$", 1") • Foam tape

INSTRUCTIONS:

Card: Cut Black cardstock $5^1/2$" x $8^1/2$". Fold to $4^1/4$" x $5^1/2$". • Cut a Map paper mat 4" x $5^1/4$". Glue the mat to the card.
Accents: Cut a Black strip $1^1/2$" x $4^1/2$". Punch a $1^1/4$" circle of corrugated paper. Affix the "A" sticker. • Flatten 2 bottle caps. Punch out 1" circles from Green and Shorthand papers. Stamp the "P" and "N" in Black and glue them to the caps. • Punch out a Tan and Blue 1" circle. Stamp the "S" and "I". Glue the circles to the metal key tags. • Use your own travel memorabilia or create labels "Espana", "Forum Barcelona 2004", and "Museu Picasso". Adhere these labels and the letter accents to the Black strip. Attach the strip to the card.

Bending an Eye Pin

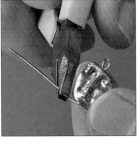 

1. Thread eye pin through charm. Using needle-nose pliers, bend ³/₈" of wire or eye pin at a 90° angle.

2. Grasp wire end with round-nose pliers and roll down forming a loop. Close loop completely after attaching to charm.

Capture that rustic 'Depression Era' look with aged images, dark brown tones, and black metals. Black bottle caps become a real asset when you need to capture this kind of imagery. This cap holds an old watch face and coordinates with black snaps that also bring back memories of old.

All The Children Card
by Judy Claxton

MATERIALS:

Design Originals Black bottle cap • Dark Beige cardstock • Dark Brown stripe • Found images (Children, Pink flower) • Checked ribbon • Small Black dress snaps • Black watch face • Small Pink rhinestone heart • *ColorBox* Pink Pastel Fluid Chalk Ink • Cotton swab • *Fiber Scraps* E-Z walnut ink • *Crafter's Pick* The Ultimate! glue • *JudiKins* Diamond Glaze • *Tombow* glue stick

INSTRUCTIONS:

Card: Cut cardstock 5¹/₂" x 10". Fold to 5" x 5¹/₂". Cut photo to fit card and cover remaining card with striped paper. Age the photo with walnut ink. Glue the photo in place.

Accents: Glue the ribbon over the seam between the photo and the paper. Glue the snaps in place. • Cut out the flower and brush Diamond Glaze over the image to adhere it to the card. Attach a watch face to the bottle cap along with the Pink heart. Apply Pink Pastel ink to the cheeks of the children with a cotton swab.

Dolls come in all shapes, sizes, and forms. This one uses interesting stickers to represent body parts.

Doll Card
by Stephanie Rubiano

MATERIALS:

Design Originals (6 Silver Bottle Caps; #1212 Art Elements Stickers) • 12 Silver eyelets • *Krylon* Silver leafing pen • Brown cardstock • Eyelet tools • *JudiKins* Diamond Glaze

INSTRUCTIONS:

Apply stickers to caps.
Fill the caps with Diamond Glaze. Let dry.
Cut Brown cardstock 6" x 9". Fold to 4¹/₂" x 6". Edge the card with Silver.
Set 3 eyelets in each corner of the card.
Adhere caps to make the doll on the front.

Little Purses

by Judy Ross

These "fat-free, no carbs, no calories" treats house small treasures. Tuck tickets and receipts inside.

Acetate Pocket Pattern

Purse Pattern Outside

Fold along dashed lines on patterns.

Hot Pink Shoe

MATERIALS:

Design Originals 2 Gold Bottle Caps • *Astrobright* Hot Pink paper • *Offray* 9" Sweet N Sour Bright ribbon • *Making Memories* 2 antique square jump rings • *Marcella by Kay* dome sticker alphabet letters • Mini clear glass beads • *C. R. Gibson* Purse and Shoe napkin • Rubber stamps (*American Art Stamps* 3 pumps; *Peddler's Pack* high heel; *My Sentiments Exactly* If the Shoe Fits; *Hero Arts* purses) • *Delta* Leaf Green acrylic paint • *LuminArte* Twinkling H20's Mystic Blue • Ink (*Ranger* Adirondack Cranberry alcohol; *Memories* Black) • *JudiKins* (Diamond Glaze; water brush)

INSTRUCTIONS:

Outside: Flatten 2 bottle caps and color them with Cranberry ink. • Fill the caps with Diamond Glaze. Add clear seed beads. Color the beads by dripping Cranberry ink on them. • Follow General Directions using Green paint. • Paint the shoes in the background with a water brush and Mystic Blue.

Stamp the *Peddler's Pack* high heel twice on Hot Pink paper. Cut out. Glue bottle caps to shoes. • Thread jump rings through the eyelets. Glue a ribbon handle to the jump rings. • Glue shoes to the lunch box.

Inside: Stamp purses on Pink paper and cut them out. Glue in place. Add acetate pocket from general directions. Add dome letters. • Cut the napkin to fit the pocket. Glue the napkin to cardstock. Slide it into the pocket.

Busy Bee Boy

MATERIALS:

Design Originals (Bottle Caps: 1 Yellow, 3 Gold; #0680 Citrus paper; #0664 School Days stickers) • Yellow cardstock • *Stickopotamous* typewriter letters • *Marcella* metal accent letters • Rubber stamps (*Catslife Press* Bee Boy; *Stampers Anonymous* Numbers collage, Stencil alphabet) • *Ranger* (Adirondack Cranberry, alcohol ink; Ice Stickles glitter glue; Markers: Cranberry, Stream, Terra Cotta, Lettuce) • Ink (*Tsukineko* Black StazOn, *Memories* Black) • *Delta* acrylic paint (Bright Yellow, Dresden Flesh, Red) • Chalks • *AMACO* Gold leaf Rub 'n Buff

INSTRUCTIONS:

Flatten the Gold bottle caps only. Color them with alcohol ink. Place School Days stickers inside. Highlight with Gold Rub 'n Buff.

Ink the Bee Boy with StazOn. Push the Yellow cap onto the face portion of the stamp. Color the image with markers. • Stamp Bee Boy twice on Yellow cardstock with Memories ink. Cut out 1 image. Apply glitter to the wings. On the other image, cut out just the body. Chalk and mount to the winged image with Pop Dots.

Follow general directions using Yellow paint. • Line the inside with Citrus paper. • Dry brush with Red and Flesh paint.

Stamp as desired. Adhere acetate pocket. Adhere number stickers to pocket. Glue bottle caps in place with E6000.

Inside: Same procedures as previous lunch boxes. Stamp Stencil alphabet and trim to fit in case. Add letters.

Lunch Box Treasures...

FAT FREE, NO CARBS, NO CALORIES!

GENERAL MATERIALS:
80 lb. White cardstock • Two 3/16" eyelets • 9" rattail cord • Assorted rubber stamps • Acrylic paints • Acetate • Pattern for acetate pocket • Paper plate • Cosmetic sponge • Spray adhesive • Vellum tape • E6000

GENERAL INSTRUCTIONS:
Copy the pattern onto cardstock. Be sure to mark the eyelet placement. • Cut it out and score. The pattern lines will be the inside of your lunch box. • Color with acrylic paints. Stamp as desired. Remember to fold the boxes so that you get the proper orientation of the stamps. • Set eyelets. • Thread rattail cording through the eyelets and knot.
Inside: Copy pocket pattern onto acetate. Score acetate on lines. Use vellum tape on the tabs of the pocket. Attach the pocket with spray adhesive. Adhere letters on pocket.

Travel Lunch Box

MATERIALS:
Design Originals (5 Gold Bottle Caps; #0669 Vintage Children stickers • *Ranger* Adirondack Terra Cotta alcohol ink • *Delta* Bright Red acrylic paint • *The Powder Keg* luggage labels • Rubber stamps (*JudiKins* hotel collage; *Hero Arts* Mexicaine; *Magenta* Air Mail) • *Memories* Black ink pad • 4" Gold ball chain • *K&Company* random alphabet letters • *AMACO* Gold leaf Rub 'n Buff

INSTRUCTIONS:
Flatten bottle caps. • Apply alcohol ink to caps. Adhere 5 travel stickers inside the caps. • Highlight with Rub 'n Buff. • Follow the general directions using Red acrylic paint. • Apply luggage stickers. Adhere pocket from general directions. Add Gold chain. • Adhere bottle caps with E6000. Let dry.

Dressing the Caps

1. Apply alcohol ink to the cap.

2. Apply the sticker.

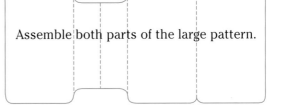

Assemble both parts of the large pattern.

The bottle cap accent contains all the colors of the beach. Check out this easy embossing technique.

Ocean Collage Card

by Laura Dehart

MATERIALS:

Design Originals (Silver Bottle Cap; #0589 At the Beach paper) • Parchment cardstock • 1 *Coffee Break* eyelet • *Fiber Scraps* Jewels fiber • *ColorBox* Cat's Eye Colonial Blue ink • Fish netting • *Top Boss* clear embossing fluid • *Lindy's Stamp Gang* Moon Glow embossing powder • *JudiKins* Diamond Glaze • Glue Dots

INSTRUCTIONS:

Card: Cut Parchment cardstock 5½" x 8½". Fold to 4¼" x 5½". • Cut the "At the Beach" paper 4¼" x 5½" and glue it to the card.
Adhere netting to the card with Diamond Glaze.
Cut a tag from the "At the Beach" paper. Ink the edges. Set the eyelet. Add fibers. Adhere the tag to the card with a Glue Dot.

Accent: Pour a thin layer of embossing fluid into the bottom of the bottle cap. Pour colored stripes of embossing powder into the bottle cap. Hold the heat gun 6" from the bottle cap until the powder melts. Let cool.
Adhere the bottle cap to the tag with Diamond Glaze.

Here's another use for small rubber stamps. These pretty accents are made by stamping warm embossing powder.

Deeply Impressed Card

by Laura Dehart

MATERIALS:

Design Originals 3 Silver Bottle Caps • *Memory Box* striped cardstock • Iridescent cardstock • 3 *Making Memories* square tags • 3 *Coffee Break* eyelets • *Lindy's Stamp Gang* Moon Glow embossing powder • Rubber stamps (*Uptown, Magenta*) • *Tsukineko* Encore Silver ink • *Stampendous* electric craft pan • *Ranger* non-stick craft sheet • Spatula • *JudiKins* Diamond Glaze

INSTRUCTIONS:

Card: Cut striped cardstock 5½" x 8½". Fold to 4¼" x 5½". • Cut a strip of iridescent paper 2" x 5½". Attach 3 square tags to the strip with eyelets. Glue the strip to the card.

Accents: Set a craft pan on low heat. Place bottle caps on a craft sheet. Fill the bottle caps with Moon Glow embossing powder. • Place it inside the pan and cover. Remove the bottle caps with a spatula when the embossing powder is melted. Caution: The caps will be HOT.
Press a Silver inked stamp into the slightly cooled but still soft embossing powder. Let the caps cool completely. • Adhere bottle caps to the card with Diamond Glaze.

Unique Projects

Turn a free-standing metal frame into an interesting memo board with travel papers and bottle cap magnets.

Memo Board with Magnets *by Susan Keuter*

MATERIALS:

Design Originals (Bottle Caps; #0669 Vintage Stickers; Papers: #0593 Hemispheres, #0594 World Maps) • *ProMag Products* Magnets • Metal Memo Board • *Suze Weinberg* Ultra Thick Embossing Enamel • Embossing ink • *Plaid* Mod Podge .

INSTRUCTIONS:

Memo board: Roughly cut paper down to size, allowing a generous overlap at the edges. Apply Mod Podge directly to the metal board. Quickly apply paper, smoothing with a brayer if necessary. Apply a generous amount of Mod Podge over the top of paper, wrapping the paper around the corners as you would when wrapping a package.

Magnets: Apply stickers to the bottle caps. Tap the stickers with embossing ink and apply 2-3 layers of UTEE. Let it cool and dry.

TIP: The magnet was not thick enough to fit properly inside the bottle cap, so I punched a 1" circle out of corrugated cardboard and glued the circle into the bottle cap. I let them set up overnight and then glued the magnet onto the cardboard circle.

Vintage Book Purse

by Erin Edelmann

MATERIALS:

Design Originals (4 Silver Bottle Caps; #0669 Vintage Children Stickers) • Old book • Matboard • Large bead • Lining fabric • Wire • Letter stamps • *Making Memories* Rub-on letters • Drill • Craft knife • Hot glue gun • *Therm O Web* (¼" Super Tape, Super Tape sheets, HeatnBond Hem Tape) • Duct tape

INSTRUCTIONS:

Prep: Remove the text block from the book cover, cutting carefully between the end pages and the cover. • Cut a piece of duct tape and line the inside of the book spine.

Closure: Drill 3 holes on the edge of each book cover. Wire a bead to the front cover.

Lining Side Flaps: Stand the book on a sheet of paper. Trace around the triangle. Add ½" seam allowance.

Cut four side flaps from lining fabric.

With right sides facing, pin two flaps together. Repeat for the other pair.

Sew flaps together. Turn the triangles right side out. Slip stitch the ends shut and press flat. • Hot glue the flaps to the spine of the book.

Purse Lining: Measure length of the purse. Add ½". Measure width of the purse. Add ½".

Cut one piece of lining to this size, press the edges under to fit the size of the purse. • Press a hem along the edges of the lining with hem tape. Add ¼" Super Tape to the inside edges of the lining.

Assembly: Apply Super Tape sheet to the center of the book covers. See diagram. Position lining. Remove backing from Super Tape in the center of the book covers, NOT along the hem. Smooth the lining fabric over the exposed sheet of Super Tape. Fold the lining away from the book edges.

Hot glue the edges of the flaps to the sides of the book covers. See diagram. Remove backing from Super Tape on lining edges. Smooth lining over flaps.

Measure the bottom of your purse. Cut a piece of mat board to this size. Check the fit by pushing it down into the bottom of your purse. Cover with lining fabric. Place fabric inside the purse bottom. **Closure and Handles:** Create a loop of ribbon to go over the bead. Thread the ribbon ends into the center hole of the back of the book and tie the ends in a knot.

Thread ribbon ends through the end holes in each cover. Knot the ends on the inside of the purse to secure.

Finish: Set stickers in 4 bottle caps. Cover the caps with Diamond Glaze. Let dry. Adhere the caps to the purse with hot glue.

Apply "destination unknown" rub-ons to the cover.

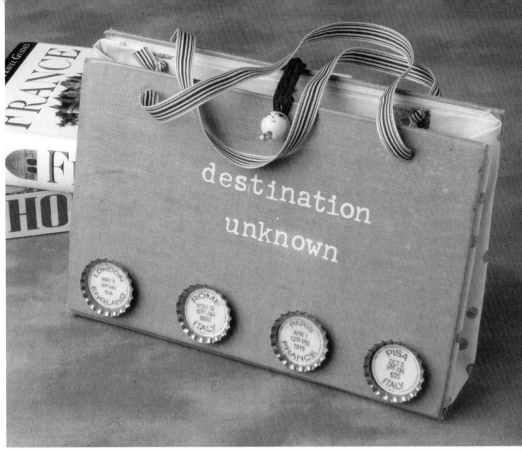

Bottle caps also make fun embellishments for altered books.

Book Purse Assembly

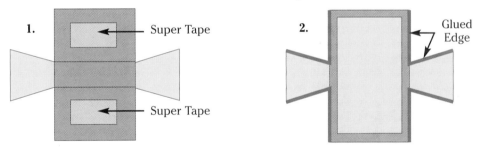

1. ← Super Tape

← Super Tape

2. Glued Edge →

Making the Book Purse

1. Trace the edges of book to make a pattern for side flaps.

2. Cut 4 side flaps from lining fabric.

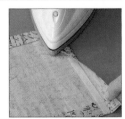

3. Hot glue flaps to the spine.

4. Press a hem in the purse lining with hem tape.

5. Smooth lining onto the book cover.

6. Hot glue flaps to the book edges.

7. Remove tape backing from the edges of lining.

8. Cover matboard with lining fabric.

simply *Beautiful*

Here comes the sun! A sunny happy face tops off this fun hanging.

Sun Window Hanger
by Linda Rael

MATERIALS:

Design Originals (7 Gold Bottle Caps; #0673 Typewriter Alphabet Stickers) • *AMACO* Maureen Carlson's "Sun" Push Mold • Air dry clay • 3 flat glass marbles • Assorted beads • 10" Gold 20 gauge wire • *LuminArte* Twinkling H2Os • *Jacquard* Yellow Pinata ink • Small nail • Hammer • Wire cutters • *JudiKins* Diamond Glaze • Super glue

INSTRUCTIONS:

Punch 2 holes opposite each other in 4 bottle caps.

Make a wrapped loop at one end of the wire. Thread the other end through the cap holes with beads in between each cap. Finish the wire with additional beads. Wrap the end and trim as needed. On 3 bottle caps, add stickers to spell "Sun". Glue these caps onto the back of the bottom 3 wired caps.

Mold a clay face to fit inside the top bottle cap. Paint with Twinkling H2Os. Let dry. Adhere the face to the cap with Diamond Glaze. Turn the cap unit over with the wired bottle caps facing up. Pour Diamond Glaze into caps. While wet, add a drop of Yellow ink, then place a flat marble into all 3 caps.

Color the back of the face bottle cap with Yellow ink.

Let dry before hanging.

Fabrics reminiscent of the Victorian era set the theme for this book.

Vintage Memories
by Linda Rael

MATERIALS:

Design Originals (Gold Bottle Cap; #0669 Vintage Children Stickers; #0679 Vintage paper) • *7gypsies* "remember" twill tape • Black rick-rack • *Making Memories* Page Pebble • *DMC* floss • White fabric glue

INSTRUCTIONS:

Flatten a bottle cap. Punch 4 evenly spaced holes around the edge of the cap. Add a sticker. • Cut a fabric to fit the front cover of your book. Cut a smaller coordinating fabric. Sew the smaller fabric to the larger one with a decorative embroidery stitch. Stitch on charms and "remember" twill tape. Sew the bottle cap to the fabric with floss. • Adhere fabric to the book with fabric glue. Adhere rick-rack to the edge of the cover.

Adhere a Page Pebble over image on the bottle cap. • Adhere Vintage paper to the inside of front cover and both sides of the back cover. • Add your favorite old pictures and memorabilia to the pages.

Artistic style makes this purse absolutely irresistible. Eye-catching images make everyone want a closer look. Create a message with alphabet stickers for a unique accessory.

Art Purse
by Kathy Martin

MATERIALS:
Design Originals (50 Bottle Caps; Stickers: #0669 Vintage Children, #0673 Typewriter Alphabet, #1212 Art Elements) • 20 feet Black 2 mm cord • 2 squares Felt 7" x 7" • 2 Ball chains 40" long • Hammer • Small nail • *Houston Arts* Omni Gel

INSTRUCTIONS:
Caps: Flatten all bottle caps. Punch a hole. Skip 4 spaces. Punch a hole. Skip 4 spaces. Punch a hole. Skip 5 spaces. Punch a hole.
Rows: Cut black cord into 5 pieces 24" long. String 10 bottle caps close together onto each cords.
Connecting rows: Cut 5 more Black 24" cords. Add cords to 5 caps as shown in diagram. This is the bottom row of bag. Fold 5 caps with 2 cords over onto the other 5 caps. String cords coming out of the bottom (the "pink" cords in diagram) in through the bottom holes and out through the top holes. Place another row of caps next to the bottom row, lining up 5 caps next to the threaded row. String "pink" cords in through the bottom holes and out through the top holes. Flip piece over so that the "blue" cords are now on the top. String the "blue" cords in through the bottom holes and out through the top holes. Repeat for remaining rows. To knot the sides of the bag, take cord out of one hole, and pass the cord from the next cap into that hole. Pull snug and knot. Start at the bottom of the bag so you will have room to tie the rows off.
Stickers: Apply stickers and seal with Omni Gel.
Lining: Sew 2 squares of felt to make a pocket. Tuck the pocket into bottle cap purse. Thread the top tails into purse top, tie off. Use thread to sew top row of caps to purse to secure.
Handle: Add a ball chain to each corner of purse.

Connecting the Purse Caps

1. Rows: Cut black cord into 5 pieces 24" long. Leaving a 5" tail at each end, string 10 bottle caps close together onto each cord so cord passes behind cap and up through the holes.

Note: cord is colored pink and blue for clarity only.

2. Cut 5 more 24" cords. Add cords to 5 caps in one row of caps as shown.

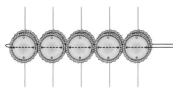

3. Fold the left 5 caps over the right 5 caps.

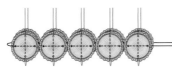

4. String "pink" cord in through the bottom holes and out through the top holes. of the 5 caps just folded over.

5. Attach next row of caps to create front of purse.

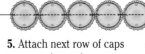

6. Fold row over to attach and create back of purse. Continue until 5 rows are completed.

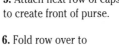

7. Tuck pocket into purse. Thread the top tails into the purse top and tie off.

8. Add a ball chain to each corner of the purse.

Even a beaded bracelet can be made more exciting by adding bottle caps with your favorite images.

Charm Bracelet
by Diana McMillan

MATERIALS:

Design Originals (5 Gold Bottle Caps; #1212 Art Elements Stickers) • Purchased beaded charm bracelet • 5 heavy jump rings • Pliers • Nail • Hammer

INSTRUCTIONS:

Flatten the bottle caps. Punch a hole in each cap. Thread a jump ring through the hole and attach it to the charm bracelet. Adhere the stickers to the caps.

If unique is what you seek, look no further. The Mona Lisa watch is an eye-catching masterpiece.

Color the Watch Caps

1. Trim edge of the image with a leafing pen to frame it and color the bottle cap with Gold. Let dry.

Mona Lisa Leather Watch
by Shirley Rufener

MATERIALS:

Design Originals (4 Gold Bottle Caps; #1212 Art Elements Stickers) • Watch face • Strip leather/suede (⅞" x wrist size plus 1½") • 2 "D" rings • *Krylon* Gold Leafing pen • *Aleene's* (Platinum Bond 7800, Leather glue) • Paper Glaze • Hot glue

INSTRUCTIONS:

Adhere a Mona Lisa image on 4 caps.
Trim the edge of the image with a leafing pen to frame it.
Color the cap with Gold. Let dry.
Glaze the images and let dry overnight.
Thread one end of the leather through the watch bars. Wrap one end around 2 "D" rings and secure with Leather glue. Taper the other end to a rounded point.
Fill caps with hot glue. Attach caps with 7800. Let dry.

Innovation

Art is creative spirit in tangible form. Next time you need a creative retreat, give yourself a chance to just do art for its own sake. You will come away energized to pursue life's challenges.

Angels Triptych
by Shirley Rufener

Dress Pattern

MATERIALS:

Design Originals (3 Silver Bottle Caps; #0672 Walnut Alphabet Stickers; #0554 Diamonds paper) • Shallow wood tray 3½" x 14¼" • 4 wing shaped found objects • 2 feathers • 3 leather scraps 3" x 3" • 1 yard fiber • 4 wood beads • *Polyform* (Art Doll Faces push mold, Premo clay: White, Ecru, Burnt Umber) • *Tsukineko* Black Versamark ink • Face stamp • *Walnut Hollow* Creative Versa-Tool • Antique glaze medium (Brown, Black) • *Craf-T* Decorator Chalks • *Krylon* Gold Leaf pen • *Kemper* 1" metal circle Pattern Cutter • Punches (½" round, square) • Paper towel • Softouch Micro-Tip scissors • *Aleene's* (Fast Grab tacky glue, Paper Glaze, Platinum Bond 7800, Leather & Suede Glue)

INSTRUCTIONS:

Box: Burn the word "ANGELS" into the wood. Burn lines on the surface edges with a Versa-Tool chisel tip. • Adhere scrapbook paper inside the box with tacky glue.

Clay: Condition the clay. Roll out a ⅛" thick sheet. Stamp 1 face with a Versafine ink and cut it out with a circle cutter. Bake as directed.• Form 2 push mold faces and bake the clay as directed. Apply glaze (1 Black, 1 Brown) to faces and wipe off the excess with a paper towel. Lightly blush cheeks with Deep Pink chalk. Adhere faces in the caps with 7800.

Angels: Arrange all angels. Color any plastic wings with metallic Gold pen. Adhere wings to the box first with 7800. Adhere the leather dress triangles with Leather glue, creating a curve at the neck and corners of the dress. Adhere cap faces using 7800. Punch round and square letters from stickers to make the words "Love", "Hope" and "Joy". Adhere the letters to the box and seal with Paper Glaze. When the glaze is dry (clear), wrap a fiber around the box and tie, adding beads to the ends with tacky glue. Tack the fiber to the box in several spots around project with tacky glue.

Making the Cap Faces

1. Press a softened piece of Premo clay into the push mold. Remove and bake as directed.

2. Roll a ¹/₈" thick sheet of clay. Stamp face with Versafine ink and cut circle. Bake.

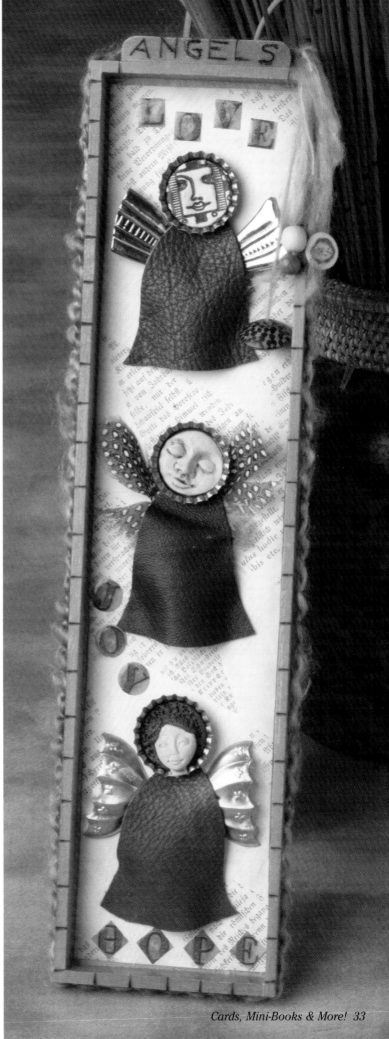

Remembering Sam

by Mary Kaye Seckler

MATERIALS:

Design Originals (Bottle Caps; Stickers: #0667 Walnut Numbers, #0672 Walnut Alphabet; #0551 Legacy Words paper) • 1 wooden frame with acrylic photo cover • Antique French text • 3 calligraphy tips • 1 antique key • 1¼" x 4" Copper glass tape • 36" Copper ribbon • spackle • ¼ c bleach • ¼ c vinegar • *Ranger* Adirondack ink (Espresso Alcohol ink, Caramel) • *Tsukineko* Bark ink • Waxed paper for burnishing • Stipple brush • Screw punch • Small butane torch • *Ten Seconds Studio* Metal Working tools • Rubber Mallet • Cutting mat • Ball burnisher dry embossing tool • *JudiKins Diamond* Glaze • *Crafter's Pick* The Ultimate! glue • PVA glue • Glue Dots • Glue stick

INSTRUCTIONS:

Cover frame: Trim Words paper to 10" square. Lay paper over the front of the frame and mark the holes for the acrylic cover screws. Punch ¼" holes where marked. Apply PVA glue to frame front. Lay paper over the frame and burnish with waxed paper.
Trim away the paper corners. Apply PVA glue to the sides of the frame and fold paper back. Burnish. • Apply glue to remaining paper flaps and burnish to the back of the frame. Edge the frame with Bark ink.
Collage: Tear 2 corner pieces from French text. Stipple text with Caramel ink. Ink torn edges with Bark. Adhere text to frame corners with glue stick.
Flatten bottle caps. Dab Espresso ink on cap edges. Insert 'Sam' and 2 decorative stickers inside caps. Pour Diamond Glaze over the stickers. Allow to dry overnight. • Mix vinegar and bleach. Immerse calligraphy tips in mixture to rust. Remove and rinse.
Lay Copper tape on a soft surface. Draw 'Heritage' letters with a ball burnisher. Decorate edges with metal-working wheels and balls & cups tools. Age metal with a torch. Peel the backing off the tape and fill the back side of the dots with spackle to prevent collapse. Allow to dry. Stick tape to the top right of the frame. Burnish gently to adhere.
Add bottle caps and rusted calligraphy tips with Glue Dots.
Wind Copper ribbon around the antique key. Glue the ribbon to the frame back with The Ultimate! glue. Allow to dry overnight. Trim the ribbon ends.

Frame Notebook

by Shari Carroll

MATERIALS:

Design Originals (Gold Bottle Cap; #0621 Children Transparency sheet; #0983 Tapes Mount; Papers: #0541 Report Card, #0549 Shorthand) • Small notebook • 1" White cardstock circle • Rubber stamps (Flower, heart, "trust your heart") • Ink (Tan, Green) • Copper Patina kit • 1" Circle punch • Sandpaper • E6000

INSTRUCTIONS:

Flatten a bottle cap. Apply Copper Patina following the manufacturer's directions. • Punch out a transparency image. Back the image with a cardstock circle and glue it to the cap.
Cover a notebook with Report Card and Shorthand papers. • Lightly sand the face of mount. Stamp the notebook with a flower in the area that will show through the mount. Adhere "imagine" and small tag to the mount. Glue the mount in place. • Glue the bottle cap to the mount.

Unity in Art

Here's a great idea - use an old key for a hanger. It matches the other metal in the project, extending the unity of the piece and adding to the nostalgic theme. Metal and sand tones give the piece a masculine look that is just the right support for this photograph.

Give a friend an artistic lift when you present this card featuring that famous mysterious smile. Add a bit of Da Vinci's genius to any project with these beautiful Mona Lisa stickers.

Mona Lisa Card
by Molly Jennings

MATERIALS:
Design Originals (3 Silver Bottle Caps; #0679 Vintage paper; #1212 Art Elements Stickers) • Cardstock (Tan, Black, Parchment) • Rubber Stamps (*Hero Arts* Manuscript; *Mostly Hearts* Eiffel Tower rubber stamp) • 2 small tags • Ink (*Memories* Permanent Black; *Encore* Metallic Gold) • Fibers • Glue

INSTRUCTIONS:
Card: Make Tan card 4¼" x 5½". • **Mats:** Cut and tear Black and Parchment cardstock to fit card front. Stamp Manuscript with Black on parchment, then again with Gold ink. Brush all Parchment edges and Black torn edge with Gold ink pad.
Accents: Cut a Black cardstock strip ¾" x 5¼". Glue in place. • Flatten 3 bottle caps. Adhere stickers. Cut out a bottle cap from Vintage paper, adhere behind the middle cap. Glue the caps to the card. Stamp 2 tags with an Eiffel Tower. Brush tag edges with Gold ink pad. Add fibers. Adhere tags to the card.

Embellished notebooks are more fun to use. They bring a bit of artistic inspiration to an everyday item. I hope you enjoy making these small projects.

Button Notebook
by Shari Carroll

MATERIALS:
Design Originals (Gold Bottle Cap; #0542 Father's Farm paper) • Small notebook • Lace ribbon • Buttons • Rubber stamps (Flower, "Timeless") • Ink (Tan, Green) • Rust Patina kit • Hammer • Nail • E6000 • Adhesive

INSTRUCTIONS:
Cover a small notebook with Father's Farm paper. • Flatten a bottle cap. Make a hole on each side of the cap with a hammer and nail. Apply Rust Patina following manufacturer's directions. Let dry. • Glue a large button in the center of the cap. • Thread lace through the holes and add other buttons. Tie the lace around the notebook cover. • Stamp the flower and word on the cover.

Link Bracelet

by Laura Dehart

MATERIALS:

Design Originals (6 Gold Bottle Caps; #1212 Art Elements Stickers) • *Rings & Things* (Split-ring jump rings, Clasp) • Circle punches (1", ⅛") • *JudiKins* Diamond Glaze

INSTRUCTIONS:

Flatten bottle caps. Mount stickers. Seal stickers with Glaze. Let dry.
• Punch an ⅛" hole on opposite sides of each bottle cap.
• Link bottle caps together with split-ring jump rings. Add a clasp.

Fun-to-Wear Jewelry

Turn a plain silver hair clip into an elegant, nostalgic bow.

Hair Bow

by Gail Ellspermann

MATERIALS:

Design Originals (3 Black Bottle Caps; #0669 Vintage Children Stickers) • Purchased hair clip • Fabric or wide ribbon • Black paint • Needle • Thread • E6000

INSTRUCTIONS:

Form the fabric or ribbon into a bow shape and sew it to the clip. • Paint the inside of the bottle caps Black. Let dry. Adhere the stickers. Glue caps to the clip with E6000.

This bracelet will tell the correct time twice a day. Make this simple accessory with your favorite sticker. It is a great project to do with a girl's group, and can be constructed in about an hour.

Elastic Band Bracelet

by Cindy Taylor Oates

MATERIALS:

Design Originals (Silver Bottle Cap; #1212 Art Elements Sticker) • ¾" wide Black elastic • Needle • Black Thread • Nail • Hammer • *JudiKins* Diamond Glaze

INSTRUCTIONS:

Flatten cap. Use a nail to make a hole on each side of the cap. Apply sticker. • Cover the sticker with Diamond Glaze. Let dry overnight or until clear. • Sew the elastic to fit your wrist, overlapping the ends. Sew the bottle cap to the elastic.

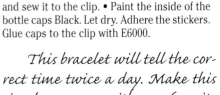

Making the Bracelets

1. Cover each image with a thin layer of Diamond Glaze.

2. Put Red Liner tape on the back of the cap.

3. Sew the caps to the elastic, adding a charm.

4. Sew clasp to the end of the bracelet.

Bracelet
by Renée Plains

If you love nostalgic jewelry, you will want to make this pretty bracelet. Collect your favorite vintage images and photocopy them.

Then, punch out the images with a circle punch. Your bracelet will be ready in no time

MATERIALS:

Design Originals 6 Gold Bottle Caps • 14 Silver star charms • Vintage images • Toggle clasp • Jump ring • ¼" wide Black ribbon 9½" long • 1" circle punch • Drill • ¹⁄₁₆" drill bit • Needle • Thread • *JudiKins* Diamond Glaze • E6000 • Red Liner tape

INSTRUCTIONS:

Flatten 6 bottle caps.

Drill two ¹⁄₁₆" holes in each bottle cap across from each other.

Punch 6 portraits from color photocopies. Remove the plastic liner from the bottle caps.

Glue a photo to each bottle cap, making sure that the drilled holes are on each side. Cover each photo with a thin layer of Diamond Glaze. Let dry.

Place a small strip of Red Liner tape across the center back of each bottle cap.

Mark the center of the ribbon and tape a bottle cap on each side of the center mark.

Sew the bottle caps to the ribbon through the drilled holes, adding charms on the front side.

Continue adding the bottle caps side by side on the ribbon.

Fold the ends of the ribbon towards the back and stitch a clasp on the folded ribbon end.

Slide Frame Necklace or Pin
by Renée Plains

If you use a bale pin back when making this piece, it can be worn as either a pin or a pendant.

MATERIALS:

Design Originals (Gold Bottle Cap; #0541 Report Card paper) • Vintage slide frame • Vintage photo • Wing charm • *USArtQuest* (Mica, Perfect Paper Adhesive-PPA) • Lightweight cardboard • Pin back • 4 brads • Flat blade screwdriver • 1" circle punch • Awl • Drill • ¹⁄₁₆" drill bit • *JudiKins* Diamond Glaze • E6000

INSTRUCTIONS:

Flatten a bottle cap. • Remove the plastic center with a screwdriver. • Punch a 1" circle with a face centered from a photocopy. Glue the photo to the bottle cap. Cover the photo with a thin layer of Diamond Glaze. Let dry. • Drill four ¹⁄₁₆" holes in a vintage aluminum slide frame ⅛" away from each corner. • Cut a 1⅞" square from mica, Report Card paper and cardboard. Glue the layers together in that order with PPA. • Use an awl to make holes in the mica/ledger through the drilled holes. • Secure with small brads. • Cut a wing charm in half at the center and glue to each side of the cap back with E6000. Glue the bottle cap to the center of slide frame. • Adhere a pin back with E6000.

1. Remove plastic liner from a bottle cap.

2. Drill a hole in each corner of the frame.

3. Use an awl to punch hole through paper and mica.

4. Insert the brads.

1. Cover a spiral notebook with paper.

2. Wrap leather around the spine.

3. Cover the leather edge with ribbon.

4. Adhere end papers inside the covers.

Books & Journals

With simple supplies, you can easily turn a purchased $1 notebook into a $20 journal. Cover the spine with a piece of genuine leather to give this journal a classic look and feel. It's a perfect graduation gift.

Travel Journal

by Gail Ellspermann

MATERIALS:

Design Originals (6 Black Bottle Caps; #0672 Walnut Alphabet Stickers; #0679 Vintage paper) • Purchased journal • Gold ribbon • Leather • E6000 • PPA • Rubber cement

INSTRUCTIONS:

Flatten bottle caps. Add stickers. • Cover the front and back of the journal with Vintage paper.
Cover the spine with leather. Adhere leather to the book with E6000. Add a Gold ribbon over the leather edge, folding to the inside. • Adhere end papers inside the front and back covers to hide the raw edges and the ribbon ends.
Adhere bottle caps to the front cover with E6000.

Concepts with Canvas

Create lovely accessories for your home with vintage photographs collaged on canvas. This is a lovely way to create a family gallery.

Vintage Collage on Canvas

by Gail Ellspermann

MATERIALS:
Design Originals (2 Black Bottle Caps; #0669 Vintage Children Stickers) • *Dick Blick* 4" square canvas • 1" wide ribbon • Buttons • Decorative papers • *USArtQuest* Mica • Lace • Color photocopies of photographs • White acrylic paint • Black spray paint • *Golden* Acrylic Gel Medium • *Ranger* Copper Stickles glitter glue • Red liner tape • *JudiKins* Diamond Glaze

INSTRUCTIONS:
Canvas: Paint the canvas White. Let dry. • Cut out photographs and adhere to the canvas with Gel Medium. Coat mica with a thin layer of Diamond Glaze. Place mica over photo.
Accents: Paint the bottle caps Black. Let dry. Edge the caps with glitter. Add stickers. • Adhere the lace, ribbon, and buttons to the canvas with Gel Medium. Adhere caps with Diamond Glaze. • Apply Red liner tape to the edge of canvas. Remove liner, cover tape with ribbon. Fold excess ribbon towards back of canvas. folding the Adhere decorative papers with Gel Medium to the back of the canvas.

Making the Collage

1. Paint the canvas a pleasing background color. Let dry.

2. Adhere images to canvas. Adhere mica to image with Diamond Glaze.

3. Adhere embellishments to canvas.

4. Wrap ribbon around the edge of canvas. Adhere paper to the back.

Smile! Here's a fun new way to use a bottle cap...in a camera flash.

Smile Card
by Judy Claxton

MATERIALS:
Design Originals (Bottle Cap; #0666 Pink Sayings stickers; 3 Black mounts; #0588 Kittens at Play paper) • Cardstock (Raspberry, Black glossy, Pink, White) • *A Little Bizaar* Cameras Collage Sheet • Small round mirror • Pink fibers • *Postmodern Design* Faces of Youth cube stamp • *LuminArte* Twinkling H2Os • *Krylon* (Silver Glitter spray, Silver pen) • White Gel Pen • *Tsukineko* StazOn Black ink • Scallop scissors • Glue stick • *Crafter's Pick* The Ultimate! glue • Mounting Tape

INSTRUCTIONS:
Card: Cut Raspberry cardstock 6½" x 11". Fold to 5½" x 6½".
Mats: Cut: Black 5⅜" x 6⅜"; Pink 5¼" x 6¼" with scallop scissors; Kittens at Play 5" x 6". • Adhere mats to card.
Mounts: Stamp faces on White cardstock and paint with Twinkling H2Os. Cut faces to fit mounts. Attach Pink braid and stickers. Set aside.
Accents: Cut out camera. Spray flash area with Silver glitter spray being careful not to spray the whole camera. Outline camera with a White pen. Glue cap, smile sticker and mirror in place • Adhere the camera to card with mounting tape. Glue mounts in place.

1. Lay transparency film over an inked stamp.

2. Press with a finger until the design is transferred.

Vintage art with Victorian flair is topped off with a bottle cap head. Check out Kathy's foolproof method for stamping on transparencies!

Daughter Card
by Kathy Martin

MATERIALS:
Design Originals (Bottle Cap; #0666 Pink Sayings Stickers; #0678 Girl Pink paper) • *Postmodern Design* stamps (Corset, Farthingale, Wooden ruler, Roses, Family Words, Block of Words) • Cardstock (Glossy Black, Yellow) • Purple paper • Black brads • Transparency film • Alcohol ink: Green, Pink, Yellow; *Tsukineko* StazOn: Black, White) • *Xyron* adhesive • Foam dots

INSTRUCTIONS:
Card: Cut cardstock 7¾" x 11". Fold to 5½" x 7¾". • Cut Girl Pink paper 5⅛" x 7¾". Adhere to card. • Stamp Purple paper with Block of Words and Black ink. Tear paper to 2½" x 7¾". Adhere to card.
Accents: Using Black ink, stamp transparency with corset, farthingale and roses. Stamp "daughter" with White. Cut out each piece as in photo. Color back of roses transparency with alcohol ink. Let dry. Run all transparencies through Xyron. Adhere farthingale to Girl Pink paper and cut out. Adhere a ruler transparency to Yellow cardstock and cut out. Adhere all other transparencies to Black cardstock and cut out. Run all pieces through Xyron. • Flatten a cap and apply sticker. **Finish**: Attach corset to farthingale with 2 brads. Adhere pieces to card in this order: Roses, Daughter, Ruler, Farthingale/Corset. Only remove sticky paper backing on farthingale from 2 bottom corners and the very top. Stick it to the card so middle part of farthingale curves away from card for added dimension. • Adhere cap with foam dots.
Tip: This transparency technique also works well with vellum and glass slides. Be sure to let the StazOn dry completely.

Turn a flower into a real beauty with a bottle cap center topped with your favorite sticker.

Beauty Card

by Diana McMillan

MATERIALS:
Design Originals (Bottle Cap; #0666 Girl Pink Stickers; #0993 Large Window Card; Paper: #0478 Green Linen, #0678 Girl Pink) • *Bazzill* cardstock (Watermelon, Petunia, Petalsoft) • White ribbon • *Making Memories* washer words • *ColorBox* Cat's Eye ink (Orchid, Old Rose, Scarlet) • *EK Success* Daisy punch • Craft knife • *Therm O Web* (Zots, Zots 3D, Memory Tape Runner) • Red Liner tape

INSTRUCTIONS:
Card: Cover the Window card with Girl Pink paper. Cut paper away from window. Ink edges of card and window opening. • Adhere ribbon below window with Red Liner tape. Adhere washer words to ribbon with Zots.
Flower: Punch out a flower from all 3 cardstocks. Ink edges of Petalsoft with Orchid, the Petunia with Old Rose, and Watermelon with Scarlet. • Cut out a stem and leaf shape from Green Linen paper. Adhere stem and leaves inside card with Memory Tape runner. Adhere flowers in a layered stack with Zots 3D. • Flatten a cap, add a sticker. Adhere cap with Zots.

No Boys Allowed! This pretty pink door hanger is "all girl".

Door Hanger

by Gail Ellspermann

MATERIALS:
Design Originals (4 White Bottle Caps; #0666 Girl Pink Sayings Stickers; #0678 Girl Pink paper) • Pre cut wooden door hanger • Pink check fabric • Pink check ribbon • Pink paint • Sharpie Fuchsia marker • *JudiKins* Diamond Glaze

INSTRUCTIONS:
Paint door hanger Pink. Let dry. • Wrap strips of fabric around top section. • Glue paper to lower section. Glue ribbon over edge of the paper. Tie a ribbon bow and adhere it to the top of hanger with Glaze. • Flatten bottle caps. Color top edge of the caps with a Sharpie Fuchsia marker. Add stickers. Adhere caps to hanger with Glaze.

Brighten someone's day with a pretty-in-pink flower, or make a bunch. Be sure to punch holes in the cap rim large enough for the chenille stem to pass through.

Too Cute Flower

by Janie Ray

MATERIALS:
Design Originals (Gold Bottle Cap; #0666 Girl Pink Sayings Stickers) • Chenille stems (Pink, White)

INSTRUCTIONS:
Flatten a cap. • Punch a hole in every space around the rim of the cap. Thread Pink and White chenille stems through the holes, forming loops for petals. • Add a sticker.

Sweet Girls

Tags are popular because they are versatile. This tag is an opportunity to experiment with collage.

Little Girls Tag
by Judy Claxton

MATERIALS:

Design Originals (Gold Bottle Cap; #0666 Girl Sayings stickers; #0585 Little Girls paper) • Large tag • Pink tissue paper • 1" square of Pink cardstock • Gold stars • Pink ribbon rose • Measuring tape • Ribbon • *Postmodern Design* Start stamp • *Marvy* Pink ink • *ColorBox* Pink Pastel Fluid Chalk • *Nick Bantock* Van Dyke Brown • *Ranger* Antique Linen Distress • *Krylon* Metallic Red pen • Hole punches (¼"; ¾") • Sponges • Cotton swabs • Glue stick • *Crafter's Pick* The Ultimate! glue

INSTRUCTIONS:

Tag: Sponge tag with Pink Pastel chalk. Stamp "start" image with Pink ink. • Glue strips of tissue to the tag.

Accents: Tear image from Little Girls paper. Age the image with Antique Linen ink. Color cheeks with Pink Pastel chalk. • Adhere image, measuring tape and rose to the tag. • Color the cap with a Red Metallic pen. • Sponge the sticker with Antique Linen and Brown inks. Apply sticker to the cap. Adhere cap and Gold stars to the tag. • Punch a ¾" circle from Pink cardstock. Glue circle to the tag. Punch a hole for the ribbon. Add ribbon.

Ribbons, fibers, fabric strips and rick-rack combine with sweet sentiments to create this darling card.

Love Card
by Susan Keuter

MATERIALS:

Design Originals (2 Bottle Caps; Stickers: #1205 Princess, #0666 Pink Sayings) • *Bazzill* cardstock (Pink, Tan, White) • *KI Memories* Stripe paper • *Doodlebug Designs* Sticker Letters • *Making Memories* (Metal Words, Date Stamp) • *Lasting Impressions* Yellow brads • Metal Corners • Fibers • White rick-rack • Gold Embossing powder • Embossing ink • *Hunt Corporation* Gold Metallic Painter • *Deluxe Designs* Card Template 9-C • ⅛" hole punch • Adhesive

INSTRUCTIONS:

Card: Cut Pink cardstock 7" x 10". Fold in half to 5" x 7".

Mats: Cut: Stripe 2½" x 3" and 1¾" x 4"; White: ½" x 2½", ¾" x 3⅜" and two 1¼" squares; Tan ⅝" x 2½" and 1¼" x 2½". • Glue rick-rack to the large Tan mat. • Punch 7 evenly spaced holes in the long White strip. Attach fibers with a Lark's Head knot. Add metal corners. • Adhere stickers to the small White squares. Add the Yellow brads. • Stamp the date on the small Tan mat and emboss with Gold. • Adhere the mats to card as in photo. • Adhere stickers to caps. Glue caps to the card. • Ink the metal "congratulations" with a Gold metallic painter to change the color. Adhere to the card.

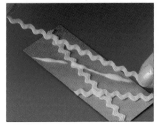

1. Glue rick-rack to a piece of tan cardstock.

2. Punch evenly spaced holes in cardstock.

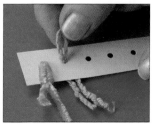

3. Attach fibers with Lark's Head knots.

Dahling, you are just going to love this card! Tallulah Bankhead was outrageous, outspoken, and uninhibited.

Make this vintage feather and lace card for the most outgoing friend you have and have a bit of fun with this old movie image.

Tallulah
by Judy Claxton

MATERIALS:
Design Originals Black Bottle Cap • Cardstock (Black, Hot Pink) • Pink and Black Diamonds Decorative paper • Lace • Ivory feather • "dream, imagine wish" Ivory satin ribbon • 3¼" x 5" Tallulah Bankhead image • Buttons (Pearl, Rhinestone) • *Posh Rainbow* ink (Metallic Pink, Rice Gold) • Corner Rounder punch • *Tombow* Glue stick • *Crafter's Pick* The Ultimate! glue

INSTRUCTIONS:
Card: Cut cardstock 6" x 11". Fold to 5½" x 6".
Mats: Cut: Black 5¼" x 5¾"; Diamond 5" x 5½". Adhere mats and lace to card.
Accents: Round the corners on the image. Adhere the image and ribbon to the card. • Flatten a cap. Apply Metallic Pink and Gold ink. • Glue the feather, cap, and buttons to the card.

This beautiful tag would make a welcome gift, tag or card. Experiment with the chalks and inks to make soft background colors. Add Ephemera images and glue them in position.

Le Jardin
by Judy Claxton

MATERIALS:
Design Originals (Silver Bottle Cap; #0529 Le Jardin paper) • Large tag • Papers (Handmade Ivory, Alphabet Script) • *ColorBox* Rose Coral Fluid Chalk Inkpad • Large button • *Making Memories* Coral twill tape • *Stickopotamus* Fleur de lis Gothic metal accent • *Krylon* Silver Metallic pen • Glitter glue • *Tombow* glue stick • *Crafter's Choice* The Ultimate! glue

INSTRUCTIONS:
Tag: Make a loop for the top of the tag by cutting 2½" of the twill and Script paper. Glue the paper to the twill. Fold in half and glue both ends to the tag. • Cover tag with Script paper. • Tear a scrap of Ivory paper and the image from Le Jardin. Adhere to tag.
Accents: Cut out "Le Jardin" word and highlight with a Silver pen. Glue twill and word to the tag. • Add the fleur de lis. • Color the cap with a Silver pen. Glue button in the cap and highlight with glitter glue. Glue cap to the tag. • Edge the tag with the Rose Coral ink.

Sweet Baby of Mine

A newborn is a delight to welcome into one's family. This cheerful card expresses all those touching sentiments and more...

Happy New Baby Card
by Sally Traidman

MATERIALS:
Design Originals (Silver Bottle Cap, #1211 Fun Faces Sticker) • Cardstock (White, Pink) • Pink check ribbon • Pink seed beads • *Mostly Hearts* rubber stamps ("happy new baby", Micro diaper pin) • Ink (Pink, Black) • Sparkle clear glitter glue • Foam dots.

INSTRUCTIONS:
Card: Cut White cardstock 5¼" x 10½". Fold to 5¼" x 5¼". • Stamp the diaper pin in Pink all over the card.
Mat: Cut a 2½" Pink square and a 2" White square. Scallop the edges of the White square. Glue the mats together. Add a ribbon loop behind the Pink mat. Adhere the mats to the card.
Accents: Stamp "happy new baby" in Black. Flatten a bottle cap. Fill rim with glitter glue and drop Pink seed beads into the wet glue. Attach a sticker. Adhere cap to card with foam dots.

Announcing a beautiful baby! This card is as pretty as your new addition to the family, and so simple to make. You will really enjoy sending these to everyone.

Pink Baby Card
by Sally Traidman

MATERIALS:
Design Originals (Silver Bottle Cap; #0666 Girl Sayings stickers)• Cardstock (Light Pink, Rose) • 1¼" Circle punch • Mounting foam.

INSTRUCTIONS:
Card: Cut Rose paper 5¼" x 10½". Fold to 5¼" x 5¼". • Punch out 8 Light Pink 1¼" circles.
Mat: Apply stickers to Light Pink circles. Glue the circles to the card.
Accents: Flatten a bottle cap. Adhere a photo inside. Adhere the cap to the card with mounting foam.

"Look at me!" Enjoy a special smile every day with this embellished frame.

Baby Frame
by Amy Wellenstein

MATERIALS:
Design Originals (12 Gold Bottle Caps; #0666 Girl Pink Sayings Stickers) • *Provo Craft* small wooden picture frame • *Darice* 1" round mirrors • *Delta* White acrylic paint • *Sakura* Hobby Crafts Crystal Lacquer • *Crafter's Pick* The Ultimate! Glue

INSTRUCTIONS:
Paint the frame White. Let dry.
Adhere stickers inside the bottle caps. Fill the caps half full with Crystal Lacquer. Glue 1" round mirrors in the remaining bottle caps. Let dry.
Glue the bottle caps to the frame. Adhere the photo.

Beaded bottle cap accents spell out the name on this pretty frame.

Embellished Acrylic Frame
by Lynn B. Krucke

MATERIALS:
Design Originals (5 Black Bottle Caps; #0678 Girl Pink paper) • 4" x 6" bent acrylic frame • Black and White photograph • 5" x 8" cardstock • Pink seed beads • *Making Memories* Heidi LC White Rub-On alphabet • Dry Embossing stylus • Craft knife • *Beacon* Glass, Metal & More glue • *JudiKins* Diamond Glaze • Double-sided tape

INSTRUCTIONS:
Frame: Cut a 3½" x 5½" window from the center of the 5" x 8" piece of cardstock. Position the cardstock frame on the decorative paper. Lightly trace around the inside and outside edges. Set the cardstock aside. Remove the center from the decorative paper, cutting around some of the bottle caps to give the frame an interesting shape. Erase any remaining pencil marks. Cut around the outside edges. • Adhere the printed paper frame to the cardstock frame. Cover with thin coat of Diamond Glaze. Let dry. Adhere the paper frame to the front of the acrylic frame.

Accents: Flatten bottle caps. Use an embossing stylus to add rub-on letters to each bottle cap. • Fill the trough of a cap with Diamond Glaze. Add beads. Let dry. • Adhere bottle caps to the frame with Glass, Metal & More glue. • Insert a photograph.

Making the Embellished Acrylic Frame

1. Cut around the bottle caps in the paper to make the frame.

2. Drip Diamond Glaze into the bottle cap.

3. Add the beads using a needle.

Elegance

Elegant and simple, this Love gift tag is very quick to make.

Gift Tag

by Sally Traidman

MATERIALS:

Design Originals (Black Bottle Cap; #0669 Vintage Children Sticker) • Corrugated cardstock • Gold ribbon • 1¼" circle punch • Foam tape

INSTRUCTIONS:

Cut cardstock 3½" x 6". Fold to 3" x 3½". • Punch a hole in the card front. • Flatten a bottle cap and affix a sticker. Mount cap behind the window. • Tie a Gold ribbon around the card front.

Patriotism never goes out of style and cards are not just for the 4th of July. Send a wonderful card as a birthday greeting to a veteran or as a statement of appreciation and thanks to a friend in the service.

Patriotic Card

by Judy Claxton

MATERIALS:

Design Originals (Red Bottle Cap; #0664 School Days Stickers) • Dark Beige cardstock • Paper (Navy Stars, Red with Navy Writing, Gold foil) • Stickers (Triple stitched flags label, Pledge) • 3 metal stars on wire (1 large, 2 small) • 4 Red eyelets • ¼" wide Navy with Stars ribbon • *Ranger* Antique Linen Distress ink • Glitter glue • Sponge • Craft iron • *Golden* Polymer Medium • *Tombow* glue stick • E6000 • Double-stick tape

INSTRUCTIONS:

Card: Cut Beige cardstock 7¼" x 8½". Fold to 4¼" x 7¼". • **Mats:** Cut a Navy mat 4" x 7". Sponge it with Antique Linen. • Adhere the mat, Red Pledge sticker, and Flag label. • **Accent:** Ink the sticker and adhere it to the bottle cap. Apply Polymer Medium to the cap sticker and flag label. Let dry. Apply Gold foil using a craft iron on a medium setting. • Set eyelets. • Cut ribbon and tape it in place. • Glue the cap over the ribbon with E6000. • Apply glitter glue to the stars. Let dry. Glue stars to the card, shaping the wire around the curve of the bottle cap.

The sticker images and Chinese coins give this bracelet an Asian flair that can be worn with any black or red outfit, or wear it with jeans and your favorite silk blouse.

Charm Bracelet

by Lisa Vollrath

MATERIALS:

Design Originals (6 Gold Bottle Caps; #0669 Vintage Children Stickers) • Purchased chain bracelet • 10 Chinese coins • 15 Jump rings

INSTRUCTIONS:

Flatten the bottle caps. Punch a hole in the top of each cap. Attach each cap to the bracelet with a jump ring. Adhere the stickers to the caps. Attach the coins to the bracelet with jump rings.

Give antique images and postcards new life by incorporating them into your art.

Vanda Card
by Judy Claxton

MATERIALS:
Design Originals Black Bottle Cap • Cardstock (Silver Gray, Black, Hot Pink) • Decorative paper • *Chronicle Books* Vanda Lotion Soap Label postcard • Silver "V" charm • White watch face • Ivory lace • Red ribbon • *Hero Arts* Old French Writing stamp • Ink (*ColorBox* Creamy Beige Fluid Chalk; *Tsukineko* StazOn Black; *Fiesta* Alcohol Magenta) • *Posh* Rainbow Metallic Silver • *Tombow* glue stick • *Crafter's Pick* The Ultimate! Glue

INSTRUCTIONS:
Card: Cut Silver cardstock 6" x 10". Fold to 5" x 6". Stamp with Old French Writing in Black

Mats: Cut a Black mat 4¾" x 5¾".Cut a Silver mat 4½" x 5½". Cut a Red paper mat 4¼" x 5¼". Adhere the mats to the card.

Collage: Tear decorative papers and layer on the card. Ink the edges with Creamy Beige. Glue the lace and papers in place. Cut the image from postcard and tie a ribbon around the image. Attach it to the card.

Accent: Flatten a bottle cap. Let dry. Highlight the cap with Silver Metallic .Glue the cap to the card.
Color a White watch face with Magenta ink. Glue it to the cap and add the "V" charm.

This card makes a fabulous gift for someone who loves to sew or quilt. Make it quickly with papers and stamps.

Red Patterns Card
by Judy Claxton

MATERIALS:
Design Originals (Bottle Caps; #0669 Vintage Stickers; #0532 Red Patterns paper) • Cardstock (Black, Ivory) • Decorative paper (Black with Dots, Black Diamonds) • Pattern tissue • *Postmodern Design* Pattern stamp • *Tsukineko* StazOn Black ink • Black check ribbon • *Krylon* Crystal Clear Spray • E6000 • Double-stick tape

INSTRUCTIONS:
Card: Cut Black cardstock 6¾" x 11½". Fold to 5¾" x 6¾".

Mats: Cut a Dot paper mat 5½" x 6½". Cut an Ivory mat 5¼" x 6¼". Cut a Red Patterns mat 5" x 6". Adhere the mats to the card.

Collage: Cut a strip of Diamond paper 2¼" x 6". Cut a strip of Dot paper 1" x 6". Glue the strips to the card.

Accents: Stamp the Pattern on pattern tissue paper with Black ink. Cut out the pattern. Adhere it to the front of the card.
Tie ribbon around the bottom of card and make a bow. • Apply stickers to the caps and glue the caps to the card with E6000.

Classy Cards

Age a black bottle cap with gold leaf to make it coordinate with the metal 'travels' plaque. The sticker and vintage paper work well to create a collage.

Gracious Lady Travels Card

by Judy Claxton

MATERIALS:

Design Originals (Black Bottle Cap; #0669 Vintage Children stickers; #0679 Vintage paper) • Cardstock: (Light Olive, Ivory) • Tags (2⅜" x 3¾"; 4½" x 6¼") • *Li'l Davis Designs* Metal Memorabilia "travels" • *Hero Arts* rubber stamps (Bon Voyage, Gracious Lady, Old French Writing) • *LuminArte* Twinkling H2Os • Fibers • Ink (*Tsukineko* StazOn Black; *ColorBox* Fluid Chalk: Olive Pastel, Dark Moss, Amber Clay) • *Krylon* Gold leafing pen • Sponge • *Tombow* glue stick • *Crafter's Pick* The Ultimate! glue

INSTRUCTIONS:

Large Tag: Cover the large tag with Vintage paper. Sponge with Dark Moss, Olive Pastel and Amber Clay. Stamp French writing with Black ink on Olive cardstock. Glue it to the tag. • Stamp "Bon Voyage" on Ivory cardstock with Black ink and ink the edges with Amber Clay. Glue it to tag.

Small tag: Stamp the Gracious Lady with Black ink and paint with Twinkling H2Os. Cut out the image and attach to small tag. • Add fibers. Glue the small tag to large tag.

Accents: Attach metal "travels".

Run a Gold pen around the edges of the Black bottle cap and attach it to the tag. Add the sticker.

If you have not yet mastered collage, this is a great card to practice with. The elements are simple and you only need one sheet of Travels paper. It's also an opportunity to play with transparencies.

Italian Ladies Card

by Judy Claxton

MATERIALS:

Design Originals (Gold Bottle Cap; #0667 Walnut Numbers Stickers; #0552 Travels paper) • Olive Green cardstock • Olive and Black Diamond paper • Transparency made from old picture • Black lace • *Hero Arts* Old French Writing stamp • *ColorBox* Dark Moss Fluid Chalk ink • Heat gun • *Tombow* glue stick • *Crafter's Pick* The Ultimate! glue

INSTRUCTIONS:

Card: Cut Olive cardstock 6" x 9". Fold to 4½" x 6". • Cut Diamond paper 4¼" x 5¾" and stamp it with Old French Writing using Dark Moss ink.

Collage: Tear images of old building and Regno D'Italia from the Travels paper and attach to card. • Place a scrap of Cream paper behind the transparency and attach to card.

Tear 2 Black diamonds from Diamonds paper. Tear a row of numbers from the Travels paper. Glue the numbers to the Black Diamonds and adhere to the card. • Attach Black lace to top right corner.

Accent: Ink the bottle cap with Dark Moss. Heat set. Adhere the cap to the card with The Ultimate! and apply the sticker.

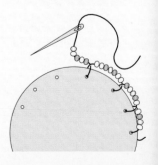

Beaded Journal

by Kathy Martin

MATERIALS:

Design Originals (4 Gold Bottle Caps; Stickers: #0672 Walnut Alphabet, #1212 Art Elements; #0679 Vintage paper) • Purchased notebook • Black waxed linen • Assorted beads • *Marvy* Matchables ink (Ochre, Brown) • 1/16" hole punch • *Houston Arts* Omni Gel • *JudiKins* Diamond Glaze • *Xyron* adhesive

INSTRUCTIONS:

Book cover: Cut Vintage paper slightly larger than the notebook. Run the paper through the Xyron. Crumple the paper to create interesting creases. Smooth out the paper. Drag an ink pad across the creases. Peel the backing off and attach the paper to the front and back of the notebook. Trim off excess.

Beaded trim: Punch holes 1" apart, ¼" from the edge of the book.

Sew beads to the book using waxed linen and a Blanket stitch.

Accents: Partially flatten 4 bottle caps. Place the Walnut letter stickers inside 3 caps. Fill the cap with Diamond Glaze. Let dry.

Apply the sticker to the last cap. Adhere the caps to the notebook with Omni Gel.

Blanket Stitch Beading Diagram

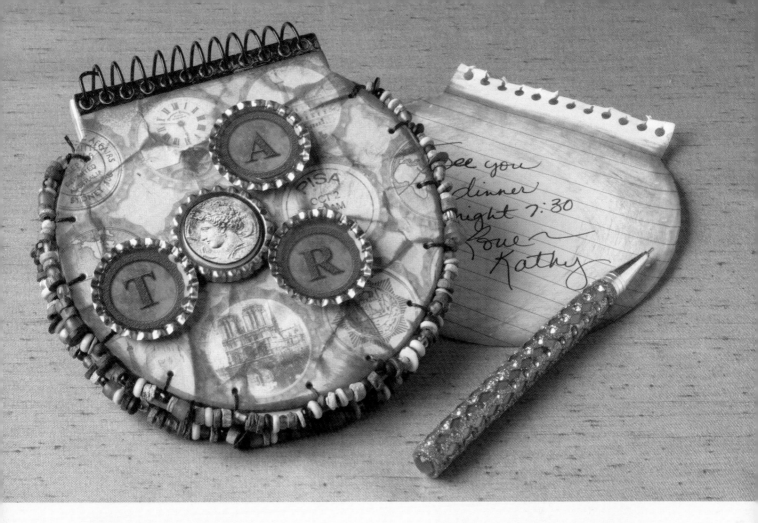

Beauty

Beautiful beaded trim around the edge adds a lot to this exquisite, yet inexpensive, journal.

Create your own line of jewelry and show off your favorite images in a charm bracelet you make yourself. It's so easy with a purchased bracelet chain and flattened bottle caps. You can even trade the bottle caps with friends.

Charm Bracelet
by Laura Dehart

MATERIALS:
Design Originals (Bottle Caps: 2 Red, 2 Orange, 2 Yellow, 2 Green, 2 Aqua, 2 Navy Blue; #0597 Fortune Cards paper) • *Rings & Things* (Link chain, Split-ring jump rings, Clasp) • Circle punches (1", ¹⁄₁₆") • *JudiKins* Diamond Glaze

INSTRUCTIONS:
Flatten bottle caps.
Punch images from Fortune Cards paper with a 1" punch.
Adhere an image inside each bottle caps with Diamond Glaze. Pour a thin coat of Diamond Glaze over each image. Let dry. Punch a ¹⁄₁₆" hole at the top of each bottle cap.
Attach caps to the link chain with split-ring jump rings.
Add a clasp.

You'll be ready for the next party with these charming drink ID's. Just open the clasp and close it around the stem of your wine glass to identify the glass as your own. This set is a great gift for a hostess too!

Cheers Drink Charms   *by Susan Keuter*

MATERIALS:

Design Originals (4 Gold Bottle Caps; #0668 Fun and Games Stickers) • *Bazzill* Kraft cardstock • Black Handmade paper • Eyelets • Loose Leaf Rings • Jump rings • *twopeasinabucket.com* Fonts (Bad Attitude, Chicken Shack) • *Fiskars* 1/16" hand punch • Staples • Eyelet tools • *JudiKins* Diamond Glaze

INSTRUCTIONS:

Charms: Punch a 1/16" hole in edge of the cap. Place stickers on both sides of the bottle cap. Fill the cap with Diamond Glaze. Let dry for 24 hours. Attach a jump ring through each hole in the bottle cap. Thread onto loose leaf rings. • **Label**: Print "Cheers! Bottle Cap Charms to Identify Your Glass" on cardstock. Cut Kraft cardstock 3¾" x 5¼". Fold to 2¼" x 5¼". Tear Black paper to fit under the fold. Glue in place. Set 4 eyelets. Staple the fold shut. Attach the charms through the eyelets.

Punch the Holes

Punch a hole with a 1/16" hand-held paper punch (or use a thin nail or sharp screw and a hammer).

Festive Drink Charms

Paris is one of the most romantic cities in the world. Celebrate the adventure with this wonderful card.

Trip to Paris Card   *by Judy Ross*

MATERIALS:

Design Originals (5 Red Bottle Caps; #0679 Vintage paper) • 2 sheets Red cardstock • Black and White checked paper • 3 Gold 9 mm jump rings • 3 travel related charms • *C.R. Gibson* Paris Poster napkin • Gold fiber • Rubber stamps (*Inkadinkado* torso; *Limited Edition* Passport; *PSX* diamond border; *Hero Arts* alphabet) • Ink (*Tsukineko* Black StazOn; *Memories* Black) • *AMACO* Gold leaf Rub 'n Buff • *USArtQuest* Matte Perfect Paper Adhesive (PPA) • Mounting tape

INSTRUCTIONS:

Bottle Caps: Stamp "PARIS" on bottle caps with StazOn ink. Flatten caps. Add holes, jump rings and charms. Highlight with Rub 'n Buff.

Card: Cut Red cardstock 7" x 10". Fold in half to 5" x 7". • **Collage**: Cut a Red cardstock base 4½" x 6½". • Tear assorted papers and napkin. Adhere to the base with PPA. • Stamp torso, passport, and diamond border onto the collage with Memories ink. • Adhere bottle caps to collaged sheet with mounting tape. Adhere collage to card with PPA. • Add fibers.